URBAN TRANSPORT APPRAISAL

STUDIES IN PLANNING

General Editors: Brian Bayliss and Geoffrey Heal

Published

Ian S. Jones: Urban Transport Appraisal

Forthcoming

Ray Robinson: The Economics of Housing and Policy

Urban Transport Appraisal

Ian S. Jones

Economic Adviser in the Department of the Environment, United Kingdom

A HALSTED PRESS BOOK

JOHN WILEY & SONS
New York

First published in the United Kingdom 1977 by
The Macmillan Press Ltd

Published in the U.S.A. by
Halsted Press, a Division of
John Wiley & Sons, Inc.
New York

Printed in Great Britain

Library of Congress Cataloging in Publication Data

Jones, Ian Shore.

Urban transport appraisal.

"A Halsted Press book."
Includes bibliographical references and index.
1. Urban transportation policy – United States.
2. Urban transportation – United States – Costs.
1. Title.
HE308.J65 1977   388.4'0973   76–54811
ISBN 0 470–99032–5

For Laurie

Contents

Preface

Brian Bayliss originally suggested that I should write a book on urban transport appraisal and has continued to give advice and encouragement in the writing of it. Others who have helped in various ways include Eamon Judge and a number of my colleagues at the Department of the Environment, notably John Welsby, Anne Marsden, Henry Neuburger, Janet Barber (especially in relation to material in Chapters 5 and 6), John Collings and Robert Anderson. Above all, my wife Janet has helped in the most practical of all ways — in transforming barely legible scripts into type.

Finally, the civil servant's liturgy. Any opinions expressed in the book are the author's own and do not necessarily reflect the views of the Department of the Environment.

Ian S. Jones

Introduction

The purpose of this book is to provide some insight into the methodology that has been developed in recent years for appraising urban transport projects and policies.

The justification for undertaking the somewhat complex set of activities involved in this appraisal is, very simply, to ensure that society is obtaining good value for money, either with respect to the resources which may be used to expand the capacity and improve the quality of the transport system, or with respect to the use which is made of existing capacity. It is especially necessary to undertake a careful examination of the merits of transport infrastructure projects, since the investment involved is often extremely long-lived. If errors are made, then society must live with them for an uncomfortably long time.

The focus of the book is primarily an economic one; that is to say, it is mainly concerned with the examination of those impacts of projects and policies to which a monetary value can be attached. Clearly there are other dimensions of impact which may be of concern to decision-makers, and some of these are considered, albeit briefly, in Chapter 11.

The kind of appraisal process which is described in the book involves, first, the assessment of the way in which people's behaviour may respond both to changes in the provision of transport facilities and to other exogenous factors such as changes in their real incomes. Second, given some specified level of the exogenous variables, an estimate must be made of the benefits which people might derive from the changes in level of provision or policy being contemplated. Third, a comparison must be made of these benefits with the costs of making the change.

Thus the term 'appraisal' covers two distinct activities, which may be labelled 'forecasting' and 'evaluation', evaluation embracing both the benefit estimation process and the comparison of benefits and costs. The organisation of the book follows this distinction. Part 1 discusses forecasting methods. Chapter 1 briefly outlines the essential elements of the appraisal process. Chapter 2 discusses the broad characteristics of the demand for transport and Chapter 3 shows how these characteristics have determined the way in which travel behaviour is analysed in broad terms. Chapters 4 – 7 then describe the components of the forecasting process in more detail. Chapter 8 shows how demand- and supply-side factors are brought together to provide the basic inputs for the benefit estimation process. Part 2 of the book covers evaluation. Chapter 9 discusses the development of the expression used to estimate benefits. Chapter 10 covers the basis on which costs and benefits are compared, whilst Chapter 11 discusses certain problems in evaluation.

Finally, Chapter 12 reviews the over-all validity of the appraisal process in the light of the earlier discussion.

PART ONE

Forecasting

CHAPTER ONE

An Appraisal Framework

It is helpful in fixing ideas to begin with a relatively simple problem confronting a highway planning authority faced with the task of deciding whether or not to expand the capacity of a road. This example is used to introduce the main elements of an appraisal framework which will be considered in more detail in later chapters. At the same time, the form of appraisal procedure here described is something of a paradigm. It may therefore also serve as a standard against which actual appraisal methods may be assessed.

The hypothetical situation confronting the highway authority is shown in Figure 1.1. The two curves, S_1S_1 and S_2S_2, represent the estimated marginal and average costs of 'producing' a journey on the existing and the improved road between points A and B and the price which the user perceives. The observed number of journeys is q, so that the point R represents a point of intersection between a demand curve for journeys between A and B and the relevant cost curves. The authority then has to estimate what the point of intersection would be on the new lower cost curve, and, if possible, the shape of the demand function between the points of intersection. Demand estimation procedures combined with information on supply-side factors thus produce an estimate of the cost and output or use levels in the after situation. Forecasts of cost and output levels with and without the improvement are then used to estimate the benefits of the improvement.

Elementary analysis suggests that the demand for travel between A and B will be affected by a number of variables other than the AB price. The most important of these are the levels of income and the size of population in the two areas; and the relative cost of moving between A and B rather than between A and B and other centres such as C and D. Changes in the level of demand with respect to changes in the first two variables will normally be positive; in the third case, demand will generally be a decreasing function of relative price.

Therefore, instead of a single demand relationship, we can imagine a

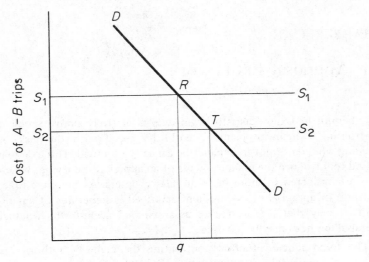

Volume of $A-B$ trips per hour

Figure 1.1

number of points such as $R_1 \ldots R_n$ and $T_1 \ldots T_n$, as shown in Figure 1.2, as being the intersection of the cost curves for the existing and improved roads with a series of demand curves which move outwards through time as income levels and the populations of the two centres increase. Conceptually, therefore an appraisal of the capacity expansion would involve a comparison of the series of annual benefits associated with the cost of the project .

Forecasts of future levels of usage, and hence of benefits, are therefore obtained in the simple model by bringing together demand forecasts and data on cost or supply characteristics. For the moment, we wish to concentrate on the demand side, and it is assumed for convenience that the characteristics of the 'supply' side are readily available.

Before examining demand estimation procedures in more detail, we briefly indicate the basis on which benefits and costs are compared.

For simplicity, it is assumed that the road improvement takes exactly one year to complete. Taking the current time period as period 0, the benefit estimation process produces a series of annual benefit estimates, labelled $B_1 \ldots B_n$, where n may be the estimated physical life of the project or some other arbitrarily chosen time horizon, such as thirty years.

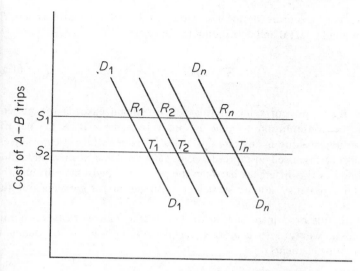

Figure 1.2

A decision to invest in a road improvement now involves society in a loss of potential current consumption, represented by the investment in the project, I, in return for a benefit stream in the form of an improved service level in the future; that is to say, the decision of whether or not to invest can be viewed as a decision whether or not to exchange gains in future consumption for the loss of some current consumption.

In considering the value for money of a potential trade-off of this kind we must be aware of the fact that for a variety of reasons individuals and society as a whole attach a higher weight to a marginal increment of consumption or benefit which accrues now than to one which occurs in the future.[1] Thus, if the marginal unit of consumption is valued at C in the current period (period 0), it will be valued at aC in period 1, where a is less than 1. The size of a is then a reflection of the rate of time preference — the higher the rate of time preference, the smaller the value of a. If the rate of time preference is constant between each succeeding pair of time periods, then C units of consumption in period 2 will also be valued at aC in period 1, and aC units in period 1 will be valued at $a(aC) = a^2C$ in period 0. In general, an increment of consumption occurring n years in the future will currently be valued at a^nC. If we write a^n in more familiar form as $(1+r)^{-n}$, then r is defined as the rate of time preference.

We may therefore define the present value of a benefit stream, P, beginning in year 0 and continuing to year n as

$$P = \sum_{i=1}^{i=n} B_i (1 + r)^{-i}. \qquad (1.1)$$

Only if the present value of this benefit stream exceeds the present value of consumption forgone in order to achieve it, is the benefit worth undertaking in any circumstances.[2] Under certain circumstances, which are discussed in more detail in Chapter 10, a positive net value (defined as the difference between the present value of benefits and the capital cost) may not be sufficient justification for carrying out the project.

With this brief introduction to the general framework of economic appraisal, we turn to a more detailed consideration of the demand-forecasting elements.

CHAPTER TWO

Introduction to the Analysis and Forecasting of Travel Demand

It should perhaps be emphasised at the outset that forecasting or prediction exercises do not necessarily involve the analysis of factors affecting the level of demand for, or expenditure on, a product or service. For example, if we have a series of figures for the number of journeys made over a series of years (for the facility in which we are interested), it may be possible to fit a trend curve to these and obtain forecasts of a sort. This type of exercise may have some utility for short-run forecasting exercises in some circumstances. In examining the possible effects of a road improvement, however, it is of very limited value since it does not show how the level of demand will change in response to the reduction in the costs of travel. At best it can provide some indication of what might be called the 'base-line' or 'do-nothing' situation. In general, it is thought useful to undertake a rather fuller analysis of the demand characteristics, and the most obvious way of doing so is within the framework of demand analysis.

Demand analysis is based on the hypothesis that the demand for a product may be specified as a function of a set of explanatory variables. The composition of the set of variables may vary according to the context in which the analysis is being carried out. For example, many demand studies have concentrated on the effects of the 'own price' of the product, the prices of a small number of complementary and substitute products, and the level of consumers' total expenditures, or incomes. In this case, the market demand relationship would be written as

$$Q_y = f(P_y, P_A \ldots P_N, E), \tag{2.1}$$

where Q_y = quantity demanded of Y, P_y = price of Y, $P_A \ldots P_N$ = prices of goods $A \ldots N$, and E = consumers' expenditure.

A most important output of this analysis is the estimated elasticity or responsiveness of demand to whichever explanatory variables are used. The elasticity of demand for Y as a function of X, E_y/E_x,[1] is defined as

$$\frac{E_y}{E_x} = \frac{d(\log Y)}{d(\log X)} = \frac{dY}{dX} \times \frac{X}{Y}. \qquad (2.2)$$

Whilst the 'full' estimation of a demand relationship may be a highly complex statistical or econometric exercise, it is sometimes possible to obtain rather cruder estimates of the elasticity of demand with respect either to price or to some other service level variable when there is a sharp change in the relative price or service level over a short period of time. This latter condition is important because other factors, such as incomes, may be assumed constant. The sudden removal of subsidies from urban rail commuter services or a dramatic reduction in travel time or cost, perhaps as a result of the kind of road improvement discussed in Chapter 1, might offer the chance to observe the responsiveness of the consumers of the services in question to a change in their relative cost or quality of service. What would be observed would be two points on a demand curve, such as R and T in Figure 1.1 (p.4), the former representing the subsidised or improved price or travel time and the latter the unsubsidised or unimproved price or travel time. Unfortunately, the information given by the two observed points is limited, and an assumption has to be made about the shape of the demand function that connects the points. Two commonly used forms are

$$q = a + bp \qquad (2.3)$$

and

$$q = ap^b. \qquad (2.4)$$

In (2.3) the elasticity is not constant at all points on the curve. In the example shown in Figure 2.1 the elasticity at A is not equal to the elasticity at B, and the midpoint or arc elasticity, defined as

$$\frac{\Delta q}{\Delta p} \frac{(p_1 + p_2)}{(q_1 + q_2)}, \qquad (2.5)$$

is often used instead. The second form of function has the attractive quality that the elasticity is equal at all points on the curve, and is the one most often used in econometric work. A constant elasticity form of function may be fitted to the two points by noting that

$$\frac{q_2}{q_1} = \frac{(P_2)}{(P_1)}. \qquad (2.6)$$

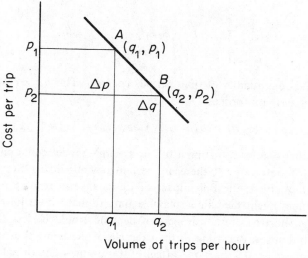

Figure 2.1

Taking logs we find that

$$\log q_2 - \log q_1 = b (\log p_2 - \log p_1), \qquad (2.7)$$

so that

$$b = \frac{(\log q_2 - \log q_1)}{(\log p_2 - \log p_1)}. \qquad (2.8)$$

If fuller time-series data are available for traffic on a particular route, then it may be possible to estimate a relationship of the following kind:

$$q_i = b_0 p_i{}^{b_1} S_{1i}{}^{b_2} S_{2i}{}^{b_3} e^{b_4 i}, \qquad (2.9)$$

where p_i = fare level in time period i, $S_{1i} S_{2i}$ = service-level variables in time period i. The term $e^{b_4 i}$ is then a time-trend variable, and b_4 would be the coefficient. If the data covers, for example, four-weekly periods, then it may be necessary to take account of seasonality by including seasonal dummy variables. The model specification would then be

$$q_t = b_0 p_t{}^{b_1} S_{1t}{}^{b_2} \ldots S_{2t}{}^{b_3} e^{b_4 t} e^{b_5 d_1} \ldots {}^{b_k d_i}, \qquad (2.10)$$

where the variables $d_1 \ldots d_i$ take the value 1 if $i = t$, and 0 otherwise.

Alternatively the model may be estimated in an annual differenced form which eliminates the need for seasonal dummy variables, specified as

$$\frac{q_{t+n}}{q_t} = \left\{ \frac{p_{t+n}}{p_t} \right\}^{b_1} \left\{ \frac{S_{t+n}}{S_t} \right\}^{b_2} \ldots e^{b_4 n}, \tag{2.11}$$

where n = the number of time periods per year. This can be estimated in point elasticity form as

$$\log q_{t+n} - \log q_t = b_4 n + b_1 (\log p_{t+n} - \log p_t) \ldots \tag{2.12}$$

Whether one is estimating a full or a simple model based on only a couple of observations, there are certain obvious difficulties to take account of. First, the full impact of the change in relative prices or travel times might take a considerable time to make itself fully felt, so that the short-run responsiveness of demand would be less than the long-run impact. Reverting to the example of the removal of rail commuter subsidies, the short-run effect of this on the usage of rail services might be very limited. In the longer term the margins of substitution open to users of the services become wider. In addition to the short-run response of changing the mode of travel between home and work (over time), the location of homes and jobs may alter, and the total level of usage may decline further. In the meantime, though, other things such as incomes are no longer constant, and the observed change in the level of usage will be due to an amalgam of factors. Crude though they are, even elasticity estimates derived from only two observations may be quite useful guides to policy-makers in certain situations.

The end-product of a comprehensive demand analysis will be a set of coefficients relating changes in the demand for the product to changes in its relative price and the incomes of consumers, and, in the case of the road between A and B, any other relevant factor such as population change. The forecasting procedure would then involve the application of these coefficients to the expected future levels of the relevant explanatory variables. However, as we shall see in the following section, the demand for transport has a number of dimensions, which may make the straightforward application of the methods of conventional demand analysis impractical.

The most important of these dimensions are as follows: (a) mode; (b) time of travel; (c) journey purpose; and (d) route.

Mode

In the simple model, the good or service demanded was a homogenous one, journeys between *A* and *B*. A more realistic specification would recognise that journeys between two points may be made by more than one mode of transport. To take an extreme example, a person travelling in a large urban area may have the choice of using as many as four different vehicular modes of transport – private car, bus, surface railway or underground railway (not counting bicycles and taxis). Each of these modes has different travel-time and cost characteristics, and the adequate specification of a demand relationship for each of them involves the difficult task of combining different sorts of units – time units and money-cost units. This in turn creates problems in the specification of a supply or cost relationship; the average cost of movement between two points depends upon the modal composition of the journeys made, so that the average-cost or supply function is no longer single-valued with respect to the number of 'journeys' made.

Time of Travel

The second dimension of travel which was not specified in the simple model is the time of day at which a journey is made. It is unfortunately not sufficient in dealing with the demand for transport simply to label the horizontal axis in terms of journeys per hour. Along with the demand for other public utilities, such as electricity, the demand for transport is highly peaked at certain times of the day. The extent of peaking is neither uniform over the transport system nor on a day-to-day basis; so, instead of a single demand curve for any particular mode, a series of demand curves are required for each discrete time period. Needless to say, the demand characteristics at each time of day may vary quite widely. Peak-hour demand, for example, may be very much more price inelastic than demand off-peak. Figure 2.2 shows the hypothetical demand characteristics for peak and off-peak travel for a public-transport mode.

Journey Purpose

The hour-to-hour variability in the demand characteristics is closely linked to another dimension of the demand for transport which again was not specified in the simple model – that of journey purpose. The

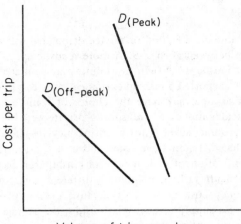

Figure 2.2

demand for transport is a derived demand, since transport is essentially an input into other activities such as work, shopping and recreation. Each of these activities creates a demand for transport, but the characteristics of these demands, most notably the time at which demand is exercised and the responsiveness of demand to changes in relative prices and income levels, may differ considerably. The hourly demand for travel between A and B at any time is therefore the summation of the demands arising from a number of journey purposes.

Route

The final complication to the simple model is that, especially in complex urban transport networks, there may be a further margin of choice open to the traveller (apart from mode of travel) – the route between the point of origin of the journey and its destination. In Figure 2.3, points $A - F$ represent the nodal points of zones into which an area has been divided for the purposes of analysis and forecasting. A journey between A and C may in this case be made directly, or via B. If points C and F had been linked, then in theory the $A - C$ journey could also have been made via F. In general, the greater the degree of interconnectivity of the transport system (for any given number of nodal points), the greater the number of alternative routes. The way in which this problem is handled is covered in more detail at a later stage.

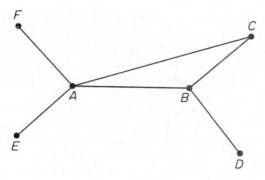

Figure 2.3

The concept of routes leads on in turn to the concept of links, since the route between A and C consists of a number of links joining nodal points. This produces another complication for the analysis of travel demand, since journeys over any particular link in the system consist not only of journeys between the two nodal points at each end of the link, as was assumed in the simple model, but also of journeys between many other pairs of points as well.

This raises the question of whether the fundamental unit of analysis in the demand for transport should be the number of person journeys using a link, for example $A - B$, or the volume of person journeys from an origin zone to a destination zone which may involve travel over more than one link. As Neuburger has pointed out,[2] the units of measurement used in the past by transport economists in specifying demand relationships have not always been very clear. There are two major arguments against the use of the link as the basic unit of analysis (and hence in favour of the journey). First, the link is in effect an input into the activity of making the journey in the same way that the journey is in a sense intermediate to the activity of work, shopping or recreation. The demand for the use of a link arises from the relative disposition of households, and the locations at which these activities take place, both of which are observable and perhaps likely to generate fairly stable demand relationships. It also arises from a number of chance or probabilistic factors such as people's expectations of the level of congestion likely to be experienced. Because of this random element, the pattern of demand or usage of any particular link may be very much more unstable than the demand expressed in terms of a movement between an origin and a destination. Second when alternative future networks are being evaluated, a link may be included in one network but not in another. In a situation like this, the evaluation procedure, operating in terms of the demand for a link or links, has to cope with the difficulties which arise when a new good is introduced.

A highly complex form of demand relationship would clearly be required to take account of all these characteristics of the demand for transport. Kraft and Wohl[3] give the following illustrative example of a demand equation for an individual living in zone i, to drive to zone j for the purpose of shopping during the period 1 (let 1 = peak and 2 = off-peak):

$$q_{ij}(A, S, H_1) = F\{t(ij)(A, S, H_1), t(ij)(A, S, H_2), t(ij)(R, S, H_1),$$
$$t(ij)(R, S, H_2), p(ij)(A, S, H_1), p(ij)(A, S, H_2)p(ij)(R, S, H_1),$$
$$p(ij)(R, S, H_2), S E_o(A, S), S E_D(j, A, S)\},$$

where $q_{ij}(A, S, H_1)$ = the quantity of round trips to zone j demanded by an individual in zone i, using mode A, for purpose S, at time period H_1; $t(ij)(M, P, H_x)$ = a vector of travel-time components associated with trips made by the individual to zone j, using mode M, for purpose P, at time of day H_x; $p(ij)(M, P, H_x)$ = a similar vector for the user travel cost components; $S E_o(M, P)$ = a vector of the traveller's socio-economic characteristics that may be associated with the mode or purpose of travel; $S E_D(j \ M, P)$ = a similar vector of socio-economic characteristics of the destination zone; A = private car; R = public transport; S = shopping purpose; and H_x = xth time period.

The market demand curve then consists of the aggregation of these individual demand curves. In practice, data limitations will normally prevent the estimation of individual demand curves, so that aggregative or probabalistic relationships using some measure of central tendency for the group as a whole are the only feasible ones to develop. This point is worth emphasising; the demand for travel consists of a multitude of individual demands, each of which is spatially specific, and therefore distinct from every other 'demand'. In analysing the demand for travel it is necessary to group sets of trip origins and destinations into zones; the degree of fineness of the zoning will depend on the nature of the analysis being carried out. Feasibility studies for an urban rapid transit system, for example, may require quite a fine system of zones; studies of the demand for the main inter-urban trunk routes will require a much coarser (aggregated) system. However, even if the analysis

is based on zonally aggregated data, some measure of intra-zonal disaggregation, for example, on the basis of household income level or car-
ownership characteristics — may make the resulting models more useful.

The existence of zones consisting of groups of origin and destination
points creates certain problems in specifying the demand for transport.
The first of these is how to deal with movements within the zone itself;
it may be that the zones are so small that intra-zonal movements, at
least in terms of demand for vehicular transport facilities, are insignifi-
cant, since many such journeys may be made on foot. The second sort
of problem is the analysis of movements between adjacent zones. In
Figure 2.4 it is obvious that the movement between the zone centroids
or nodal points O_1 and O_2 is only a crude proxy for a movement from
point A to point B, or from point C to point D, to take two extreme
cases. Once again, much depends on how finely the zones are defined,
which will depend upon the sort of analysis that is being undertaken.

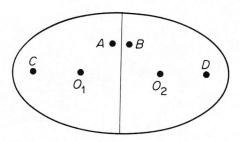

Figure 2.4

One final problem is how to deal with transport movements which
begin and/or end outside the closed area within which the demand for
transport is being analysed. In most large urban areas, the proportion
of such movements forms only a very small proportion of total traffic
movement (for very large urban areas with populations of 1 million or
more, it may be as low as 2-5 per cent),[4] and in practice some sort of
ad hoc arrangement is usually made for dealing with such movements.

It should be clear enough that the quantity of data required for a
comprehensive analysis of travel demands along the lines of orthodox
economic demand analysis would be enormous, as Kraft and Wohl
recognise.[5] What they fail to point out, however, is that the data
required for orthodox demand analysis is different in kind from that
obtained from surveys carried out at a particular point of time. Demand
studies have usually relied upon time-series data, so that the effects of

relative price changes on the demand for the good or service may be studied. Information on income – consumption patterns available from cross-section data may of course be used as a check on the income-elasticity estimates derived from the analysis of the time-series data. The essentially cross-sectional nature of the data most often used in analysing the demand for transport in practical studies would suggest that such studies may be relatively weak on the subject of price responsiveness in the system, and this is indeed the case. This point is taken up in the following chapters, which deal with the procedures for analysing and forecasting the demand for transport developed in urban transport studies.

CHAPTER THREE

Some Alternative Approaches to the Analysis of Travel Demands

Chapter 2 outlined some of the characteristics of travel demand which are relevant for its analysis. We now show how these characteristics have influenced the analysis of demand. The intention is to give a brief overview of the components of a framework within which demand and demand – supply interaction may be examined in advance of the more detailed discussion in subsequent chapters.

In Chapter 2 it was argued that the primary unit of analysis in the transport planning context should be the total of zone-to-zone person journeys disaggregated by journey purpose, mode of travel and time of day. The starting point for an analysis of travel behaviour is therefore the division of the planning area into a set of zones. Next, the transport network must be represented and the zoning system linked up to the network so that routes may be specified between zone pairs.

The zoning system is usually devised so that the type of development, such as residential or commercial, is relatively uniform within each zone. The size of zone tends to be a function of the density of development within the zone, so that zone size generally increases away from the centre of the urban area.

Data on travel patterns within an area during a specified time period are obtained from surveys of households, and industrial and commercial establishments. Traffic counts of various kinds may be used as a check on the reliability of the survey information. The analytical process then seeks to explain the observed pattern of trip-making as a function of two sets of variables, land-use characteristics and transport-network characteristics.

Land-Use Characteristics

The most important of these are as follows:

(a) the socio-economic characteristics such as size, income and car-ownership levels of the households resident in the zone;

(*b*) the number of employment opportunities in the zone;

(*c*) shopping and commercial floor space in the zone, and

(*d*) number of school places in the zone.

Clearly not all of these characteristics of land use in a zone are relevant to each journey purpose. For example, if we wished to examine the pattern of trips from home to school, then we would concentrate on the household characteristics at the origin end and the number of school places at the destination end. The residential land use is generally treated as the generator of trips, whilst the other land uses are thought of as attractors. Journeys to and from home form the majority of person journeys and are described as 'home-based'. Journeys with the home as neither the origin nor the destination are described as 'non-home-based'.

Transport-Network Characteristics

The highway network used in the planning process is not a full description of an area's actual highway network. Instead, only major roads are identified and represented in the modelling network. Each zone in turn is represented in 'network space' as a single centroid which is attached to the set of links at nodal points as shown in Figure 3.1.

Here *A – F* represent zones. The main network links are represented

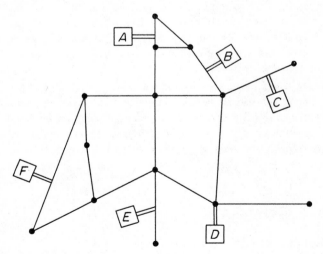

Figure 3.1

by the single lines. The links between the main networks and the zone centroids are shown as double lines. These are known as 'connectors', and are inserted to represent the fact that trips may begin and end at points which do not lie on the main network. The main links themselves are described in terms of their length and performance characteristics. On the basis of this network, a set of minimum time or cost routes between pairs of nodal points (zones) can be defined; this can be simply expressed in terms of a minimum travel-time or cost matrix as shown in Figure 3.2. Any element in the matrix, say the ijth, then represents the cost or time of travel from zone i to zone j. Two points to notice about the matrix are, first, that the elements of the leading diagonal showing the intra-zone costs are non-zero, and, second, that the matrix is square rather than triangular — implying that the $i-j$ cost or time is not necessarily equal to the $j-i$ cost or travel time. A set of such matrices may be defined for each travel mode and even for peak and off-peak travel by mode.

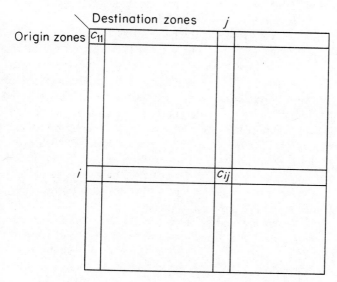

Figure 3.2   A travel cost matrix

Alternative Approaches to the Analysis of Travel Demand

As indicated in Chapter 2, the simultaneous determination of a set of demand relationships would require very large quantities of data and a set of models which could be used to explain both travel behaviour and the interaction between travel demand and location. Transport planning methodology has generally assumed away the problem of land-use – transport interaction in the forecasting context by examining the effects of alternative transport measures given a fixed set of land uses. Since the adjustment of land use to changes in the transport system is likely to be important only in the rather long term, this may be a valid simplification, especially when the planning process is examining short-term policy options.

Even when operating within a constraint of fixed land uses, the analysis of travel behaviour still has to cope with the complexities which stem from the simultaneous nature of transport decision-making. This involves choices with respect to the following:

(*a*) whether or not to travel (trip generation);

(*b*) where to travel to (trip distribution);

(*c*) by which mode to travel (modal choice);

(*d*) by which route to travel (assignment); and

(*e*) when to travel.

The final margin of decision, when to travel, has not been as extensively analysed as the first four elements in any of the alternative structures within which travel demand has been analysed.[1] In justification it can be argued that, in practice, certain important types of trip (such as those to and from work – except when some kind of flexible working-hours system is in operation – and school) do not have an effective choice of when to travel. However, the transport planning process may be required to examine policy options which involve an increase in peak – off-peak travel-cost differentials (in favour of off-peak travel). An assessment of the potential efficiency gains from such policies involves estimating the degree to which trips might switch from peak to off-peak. The lack of this facility must therefore be counted as a handicap of existing models. Having said this, it should be emphasised that, even if model structures could be adapted to incorporate time-diversion effects, prediction would continue to be handicapped by a lack of firm empirical evidence on responses to increased peak – off-peak cost differentials.

A further point to notice is that choice of route is not usually analysed as a 'pure' demand-side decision. Assumptions about route choice are built into the earlier stages of analysis, generation, distribution and model choice, and the assignment stage itself can be represented in terms of an interaction between demand- and supply-side factors. This is discussed in more detail in the final part of this chapter and in Chapter 8 on assignment.

There are two main alternative approaches to the analysis of travel demand, neither of which fully represent the several margins of decision open to the consumer. In the remainder of this chapter we briefly outline what these alternatives are, and the main points of difference between them.

Direct Demand Analysis

The first method of analysis is known as the 'direct' or single-stage model (following Manheim).[2] Here the volume of trips between zone pairs such as i and j by mode k is estimated in a single stage as a function of land-use and transport-network variables. In other words, models of this kind simultaneously represent behaviour with respect to trip generation, trip distribution and mode choice in a single demand relationship — usually of the form shown in equation (3.1):

$$T_{ijk} = f(G_i, A_j, C_{ijk}, C_{ijm}),   \text{(3.1)}$$

where T_{ijk} = volume of $i-j$ trips by mode k; G_i = land-use variables relating to origin zone i; A_j = land-use variables relating to destination zone j; $C_{ijk} = i-j$ travel cost by mode k; and $C_{ijm} = i-j$ travel cost by mode m. Equation (3.1) may also be written with mode-specific trips per head of origin-zone population, as in equation (3.2):

$$\frac{T_{ijk}}{P_i} = f(G_i, A_j, C_{ijk}, C_{ijm}),   \text{(3.2)}$$

where P_i = population of origin zone i. Both the 'absolute' and *per capita* forms of the direct model may be estimated by means of multiple-regression methods, using either data from a full travel matrix (of the kind shown in Figure 3.2) above or from a single row or column of the full matrix. In the second case the (*per capita*) model would be estimated in the following form:

$$\frac{T_{ijk}}{P_i} = f(A_j, C_{ijk})   \qquad \text{(single origin)}   \text{(3.3)}$$

or

$$\frac{T_{ijk}}{P_i} = f(G_i, C_{ijk})   \qquad \text{(single destination).}   \text{(3.4)}$$

Mansfield,[3] for example, used a model of the form given by equation (3.4) to examine recreational trip patterns.

The best known example of the many-origin – many-destination direct model is the so-called 'abstract' (or 'attribute') mode model developed by Quandt and Baumol.[4] This model explained mode-specific trip volumes between pairs of urban areas as a function of socio-economic and land-use characteristics of the areas, and the performance characteristics of the competing modes. The 'modal' aspects of the model are of particular interest. Service-level characteristics such as out-of-pocket costs, speed (or travel time) and departure frequency were specified for each mode. Demand for any mode, k, was then a function of the absolute performance of the 'best' mode, taking each service-level characteristic into account, and of the performance of mode k relative to the 'best' mode. The general form of the model may therefore be written as

$$T_{ijk} = f\left\{G_i, A_j \sum_i \left(x_{ijb}^i, \frac{x_{ijk}^i}{x_{ijb}^i}\right)\right\}, \tag{3.5}$$

where x_{ijb}^i, x_{ijk}^i = performance levels of best (b) and kth mode with respect to service-level variable i.

The original work by Quandt and Baumol also included a variable relating to the number of alternative modes available on a route. Incorporation of a variable of this kind involves certain conceptual difficulties, in particular those relating to the definition of modes which have not been satisfactorily resolved (this problem is taken up again in Chapter 7 on modal choice). Another problem specific to the form of model given by equation (3.5) is that demand for mode k is related only to its performance characteristics and to those of the 'best' mode. A formulation of this kind does not allow for competition between 'inferior' modes.

Relatively few examples exist of direct-model estimation in the urban context. Domencich, Kraft and Valette (DKV) have estimated a model for urban shopping trips by public transport, taking the general form shown by equation (3.1) above.[5] Generation (G_i) variables were household numbers (H_i), average household size (N_i) and average household income (Y_i) in zone i. Attraction variables were zone j's total employment (E_j), it's share of total retail employment in the region (S_j) and its share of employment in personal business activities in the region (T_j). Modal variables were out-of-pocket costs (c) and trave times (t) for public transport and car. The model was estimated in the following form:

$$T_{ijk} = b_0 H_i^{b_1} N_i^{b_2} Y_i^{b_3} E_j^{b_4} S_j^{b_5} T_j^{b_6} C_{ijk}^{b_7} t_{ijk}^{b_8} C_{ijm}^{b_9} t_{ijm}^{b_{10}},$$

$$(3.6)$$

so that the parameters $b_1 - b_{10}$ were elasticity estimates. Interestingly, neither of the two cross elasticity coefficients (b_9 and b_{10}) were significantly different from zero, implying a high degree of market separation between car and public-transport modes.

The DKV model can be straightforwardly re-expressed in terms of trips per household. This might indeed be necessary for estimation purposes if there is not significant variation in the number of households per zone. On the other hand, if there is significant variation, then the effect of zone size on trip flows may 'swamp' the effect of other variables.

Despite the apparently large number of variables, the DKV model's treatment of the factors affecting trip generation and modal choice is relatively crude. Thus the DKV model is estimated on the basis of zonal average data with respect to household characteristics. Yet subsequent work on trip generation discussed in more detail in Chapter 4, has shown that a major part of the variation in trip-making rates occurs within rather than between zones. This work has also pointed to the separate importance of household-structure and car-ownership factors which are not included in the DKV form of model. Similarly, work on modal choice has demonstrated the significance of service-level characteristics such as access and wait time which the DKV model does not include. This work also suggests that better results may be obtained by an initial disaggregation of the household population into car-owning households and non-car-owning households (the latter having no effective choice of vehicular mode in most areas). Yet it may be appreciated that a regression-based model which attempts to include all of these factors in a simultaneous treatment may lack robustness (in the sense of having high standard errors on the estimated coefficients) because of collinearity between the explanatory variables.

Finally, the direct model does not explicitly allow for competition between alternative destination zones. The only land-use and network service level variables included in equation (3.1) relate to zones i and j. In this formulation, therefore, changes in land uses in zones other than i and j or in travel costs from zone i to other zones will leave ijk trip volumes unchanged. It follows that, using the direct model, the forecast change in the total volume of trips made in an area is simply the sum of the forecast changes in mode-specific trip volumes between each pair of zones in the area. It is in this respect that the direct model stands in strongest contrast to the usual form of sequential model which provides an alternative approach to the analysis of travel demands.

Sequential Demand Analysis

The sequential form of analysis examines the demand for travel in a number of stages, each of which is self-contained. The first stage analyses the number of trips originating and ending in each zone. In principle this would be explained as a function of land use and the level of service provided by the transport network. However, in most work on transport planning, trip generation from zone i is expressed only as a function of land use in the zone. The result is that the elasticity of total trip-making from i with respect to network costs, which we may define as

$$\frac{C}{O_i} \times \frac{\partial O_i}{\partial C}, \qquad (3.7)$$

where O_i = trip origins at i and C = some measure of network service level, is zero.

The second stage of the analysis involves the distribution of the O_i trips amongst the set of alternative destination zones. In the most familiar type of gravity formulation, trips from i to j are a function of the attractiveness of j relative to other zones, as reflected in its land-use characteristics and travel costs. Thus T_{ij} may be written as

$$T_{ij} = \{O_i \, f_1(A_j) f_2(C_{ij})\} \, \{ \sum_j f_1(A_j) f_2(C_{ij}) \}^{-1}. \qquad (3.8)$$

In a formulation of this kind explicit account is taken of the competition provided by alternative destinations so that the cross-elasticity terms defined $(\partial T_{ij}/\partial C_{im}) \times C_{im}/T_{ij}$ are non-zero.

The third stage in the sequential process involves the allocation of the T_{ij} trips between alternative modes on the basis of their respective travel costs. Thus the share of T_{ij} trips obtained by mode k may be written as

$$T_{ijk} = T_{ij} \{f(\sum_k C_{ijk})\}. \qquad (3.9)$$

In some more recent studies, the modal-split and distribution stages have been combined into a single stage.

In addition to the distinction between 'direct' and 'sequential' analyses of travel demand, it is also possible to separate out studies which examine each of the dimensions of demand, and those which are confined to a single aspect. 'Partial' models of this latter kind have been used most frequently in the analysis of mode choice, and are discussed in more detail in Chapter 7. Finally, a distinction may also be made between models which operate with aggregative — usually zonal — data, and those which operate with disaggregative — household — data. This distinction is significant in the analysis of trip generation and modal choice.

As has been pointed out, both the direct and sequential forms of demand model explain the demand for travel in terms of land-use and transport-network variables. In this formulation, the transport-network characteristics are equivalent to the set of prices in the conventional demand analysis. We now examine briefly the process by which an equilibrium of output and price of service is obtained in the analysis of transport networks.

We start from the most straightforward case, where demand for each product is a function of own price (P) and a set of exogenous factors (E) such as income. Supply is expressed simply as a function of the price of the product. Thus

$$
\left.
\begin{aligned}
(a) \quad & D_i = f_1\,(P_i, E) \\
(b) \quad & S_i = f_2\,(P_i) \\
(c) \quad & D_i = S_i
\end{aligned}
\right\} \quad \text{for all } i. \qquad (3.10)
$$

Alternatively it is sometimes convenient to write the demand and supply relationships slightly differently; thus

$$
\begin{aligned}
(a) \quad & P_i = f_1\,(Q_i, E) \\
(b) \quad & C_i = f_2\,(Q_i) \\
(c) \quad & P_i = C_i.
\end{aligned}
\qquad (3.11)
$$

Here the demand function is written as an average-revenue function; the supply function is written as a cost function.

In each case, however, a system of three equations in three unknowns is defined, and a solution may be obtained for whatever level of the exogenous variables is specified, given the normal forms of the functions concerned.

As soon as the assumption of independent demands is relaxed, the problem of finding a solution becomes immensely more complex (except under certain supply or cost conditions). We have already indicated that the independence assumption cannot be applied to the basic unit .of transport demand; the position is made even more complex, however, since the 'supply'-side relationship for each *ijk* element depends upon the output levels of other *ijk* elements. This follows from the definition of a transport network in terms of a set of links, each of which may be used by journeys between many *ij* pairs and by more than one mode. The demand – supply framework in this case may be specified as follows (the specification is as per equation 3.11):

$$(a) \quad P_{ijk} = P(T_{ijk}, \ \sum_j \ \sum_k \ P_{ijk}, E_i, \ \sum_j E_j)$$

$$(b) \quad C_{ijk} = C \ (\sum_x \ \sum_y \ \sum_z \ T_{xyz}) \qquad (3.12)$$

$$(c) \quad P_{ijk} = C_{ijk},$$

where $\sum_x \sum_y \sum_z T_{xyz}$ = the set of trips between zones x and y by modes which may use links traversed by *ijk* trips, and E_i, E_j etc. = exogenous (land-use) variables.

For the system as a whole, the number of equations equals the number of unknowns so that it is soluble in principle, given certain restrictions on the relevant functional forms. However, each individual set of equations contains more unknowns than equations. The solution process must therefore be iterative, with trial values assumed for the prices and output levels other than the *ijk*th one.

The distribution and modal-split stages of the sequential process (and the direct model) usually employ a set of 'trial' values for the price set, and therefore imply some specific level of use of each link in the network. Supply – demand interaction is then usually confined to the assignment stage, when the trips predicted by the earlier stages of the demand analysis are assigned to the network. The pattern of *ijk* costs produced by the assignment process may very well not be the same as the set of *ijk* costs used in the demand analysis. This is illustrated in Figure 3.3. The cost used to distribute trips is represented by P_{ij}^0. The level of *ij* costs which results from the assignment of t_{ij}^0 trips to the network is P_{ij}^1. At this level of costs, the volume of trips predicted by the demand relationship would in fact be t_{ij}^1.

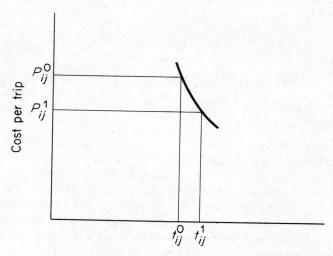

Volume of $i-j$ trips per hour

Figure 3.3

This apparent inconsistency suggests that there is a need for some iteration back from the assignment stage to the demand-forecasting process. In practice, this iterative process is often ignored in the sequential analysis. To undertake it would be extremely cumbersome in terms of the computing requirements, given existing technology. One advantage of the direct, or single-stage, demand estimation process is that it allows demand-supply interaction to take place more easily.

The following chapters discuss the sequential analysis of travel demand in more detail. This is not because of any strong conviction that this form of analysis is superior to the direct form, but simply because the sequential process currently provides the basis for much urban transport planning work. It therefore provides a standard against which alternative approaches may be examined. Some further comparisons of the different approaches will be made, especially in Chapter 6 on trip distribution.

CHAPTER FOUR

The Analysis and Forecasting of Trip Generation and Attraction

The analysis of trip generation and attraction is the first stage in the sequential approach to travel demand forecasting. The inclusion of the term 'attraction' requires some explanation since the outline discussion in Chapter 3 only introduced the concept of 'trip generation'. In fact, the analysis of trip attractions is entirely equivalent to the analysis of trip generation. That is to say, it examines the number of trips attracted to a zone (for some specified journey purpose) as a function of zonal land-use characteristics. It is required as an input to the process of forecasting future trip-making by means of the so-called 'doubly constrained trip distribution model', whose characteristics are discussed in more detail in Chapter 6.

The theoretical foundation of much traffic analysis and forecasting work is the book by Mitchell and Rapkin, *Urban Traffic – A Function of Land Use*.[1] Following Mitchell and Rapkin, early work on the analysis of trip generations related trip-making to broad land-use categories, such as residential, industrial and commercial, and separate trip-making rates were estimated for each category. Initially such analysis used a very simple regression-based approach, relating trips generated to variables such as the number of households per zone (residential zones), the industrial floor space (industrial zones), or retail sales area (commercial zones). The deficiencies of this approach are apparent; in the case of residential zones, the use of a simple 'number of households' variable is unlikely to explain a great deal of the variance in zonal trip-making rates, reflecting the varying characteristics of the households living in the zone, such as their size, their income, their car-ownership levels, or the accessibility of the zone to other parts of the area. Accordingly, analysis of trip generation has focused on the household as the fundamental unit of analysis; some work has used exclusively 'household' variables such as income levels and car-ownership rates. Other work has incorporated 'zonal' characteristics, such as residential density or distance from the urban centre (C.B.D. in North American parlance), which are perhaps designed to proxy 'transport-network' factors.

There have been three alternative approaches to the analysis and forecasting of household trip generation, distinguished first by the level of disaggregation applied to the data, and second by the choice of statistical technique employed in the analysis.

Regression-Based Approaches

There have been two variants of the regression-based approach to trip-generation analysis:

(*a*) analysis in terms of the zonal averages of the chosen explanatory variables using multiple-regression techniques; and

(*b*) analysis in terms of individual household data also using multiple-regression techniques.

These two approaches can be compared in terms of the data inputs to the formal regression model:

$$Y = Xb + u. \tag{4.1}$$

In the zonal average approach, Y is an $N \times 1$ column vector of average trip-generation rates (total or purpose-specific) for the set of n zones into which the survey area has been divided; X is an $N \times K$ matrix of zonal averages of the K household characteristics used as explanatory variables. In the second approach, Y is an $M \times 1$ column vector of the trips generated (total or purpose-specific) by the M households for which data are available; X is the $M \times L$ matrix of the L explanatory household characteristics. The zonal total trip origins necessary as an input to the travel forecasting exercise may be obtained by inserting zonal average figures of the explanatory variables.

The merits of these alternative approaches have been quite extensively discussed in the existing literature. The first point which comparative studies of the two approaches have emphasised is that the relative importance of certain explanatory variables used in the analysis (in particular, household size) varies widely between the two methods. That is to say, the estimate of the value of the coefficient relating trip generation to household size in the analysis of individual household data is different from (and usually greater than) the value of the coefficient obtained using zonal average data. It has been shown by Oi and Shuldiner that household size is an important explanatory variable in the analysis of individual household trip-making rates,[2] even when used alongside other variables such as car-ownership rates. On the other hand, in analysis carried out at the zonal level, the zonal average household size variable tends to add very little to the degree of explanation achieved by other variables, most notably car-ownership and income levels. The main reason for this is that the spread of zonal average household sizes is a relatively narrow one, compared to the spread of other explanatory variables.

More generally, the use of any zonally averaged or grouped data produces sets of variables with substantially less variability than non-grouped data. In trip-generation work reported by Fleet and Robertson,[3] for example, nearly 80 per cent of the variance of total trip-generation rates was within zones. Not surprisingly perhaps, in Fleet and Robertson's work, the fit of the regression equations using zonal average data was substantially better than the fit of the individual household data (an R^2 of 0.95 against 0.36). However, the authors went on to show that this apparent superiority was somewhat misleading. They did so by combining the zonal average values of the explanatory variables with the coefficients derived from the household equation. The degree of explanation of zonal variance of this composite model was then very little different from that achieved in the model fitted to zonal average values. The choice between the two levels of aggregation must depend both upon the goodness of fit achieved, and upon the robustness of the relationship if it is to be used for forecasting purposes. If the major point of difference between the zonal average and household approaches is over the significance attached to the household-size variable, then if either method is able to achieve a comparable degree of explanation, the choice between them should depend upon the expected stability of the relationship concerned and on the reliability with which forecast values of the explanatory variables can be obtained.

Thus if changes in the size distribution of households or in the average household size within zones are expected, then the use of zonal average data for forecasting purposes carries more risk.

Oi and Shuldiner have made two other observations about the use of regression models in the analysis of trip generation, both at a zonal average and at the household level. The first is that there may be quite high correlations between the different variables used to explain household trip generation in the linear regression model. For example, in the analysis of household trip-making, an estimating equation of the following kind may be used:

$$T = b_0 + b_1 H + b_2 O + b_3 Y + u, \qquad (4.2)$$

where T = from-home trips, H = household size, O = car-ownership level (expressed either as a rate per zone in the case of analysis at the zonal level, or as a dummy variable taking the values 0, 1 or 2, for example, if individual household data is used), and Y = income level.

Examination of the correlation matrix usually reveals high positive correlations between O and Y; Oi and Shuldiner, for example, obtain an R of $+0.6$ using zonal average data.[4] In these circumstances, it is clearly difficult to decide which is the true determining variable. One way of dealing with the problem would be to construct a fully specified model, in which the car-ownership rate, for example, appeared as an endogenous variable. It is for this reason that the introduction of 'zonal' characteristic variables, such as residential density or distance from the C.B.D. may not significantly improve the fit of models in which car ownership, income or even household size are already included as explanatory variables. An example of this, again drawn from the work of Oi and Shuldiner, is the high correlation between car-ownership level and distance from the C.B.D.,[5] on the other hand, in the analysis of individual household data, the authors found a rather low correlation (only 0.09) between C.B.D. distance and car-ownership levels.[6]

The second point made by Oi and Shuldiner is that the relationship between the variable to be explained and the explanatory variables may be non-linear if the latter are expressed in arithmetic terms. This emerges most clearly in their analysis of individual household data in which they examined the effect of increasing car-ownership rates and household size separately on trip-making with the other variable held constant. The results, using data from the *Detroit Area Transportation Study*, are shown in Table 4.1.[7]

TABLE 4.1

Mean number of total trips per dwelling unit classified by car ownership and household size (Detroit 1955)

Persons per dwelling unit	Number of vehicles per dwelling unit			
	0	1	2+	Total
1 and 2	1.71	5.09	6.68	4.00
3	3.32	6.92	8.82	6.93
4	3.40	7.63	11.28	7.91
5 or more	4.12	9.05	13.15	9.55
Total	2.40	6.93	10.58	6.64

Oi and Shuldiner do not themselves go further than to point out the difficulties produced by non-linearities in the relationships, and to test some (arithmetically) non-linear forms of estimating equations. However, their work contains two important pointers to an alternative approach to the analysis of household trip generation. First, it suggests that the major sources of variation in household trip-making are household structure and household car ownership. The only dimension of structure actually examined by Oi and Shuldiner was the number of persons per household. *A priori* expectation would be that the number of employed persons per household would also be a significant explanatory variable, operating independently of total numbers in the household. There are two potentially useful types of interrelationship not fully examined by Oi and Shuldiner which suggest how a household trip-generation model might be structured. First, household-survey evidence suggests that mean income per household is an increasing function of the number of persons employed per household. Second, it would appear that car ownership can be treated endogenously as a function of household income and structure. Taken together, these observations suggest that the analysis of household trip generation should first of all examine the joint distribution of households by structure type and income, and the inter-zonal distribution of households with specified income-structure characteristics. Household car ownership could then be estimated as a function of the structure and income variables, and possibly of residential density — although, as Oi and Shuldiner point out — this latter variable may itself be highly correlated with the household-income variable. In a forecasting context, the first objective would then be to predict the distribution within and between zones of households classified by household structure and income. Car ownership would then be estimated for each household income-structure category using appropriate estimating relationships.

Second, instead of regression-based approaches, Oi and Shuldiner's work suggests that if households can be classified on the basis of those variables which are the main source of variation in household trip-making, it may be possible to analyse household trip-making in terms of the average value for a household category, such as the value shown for a two-person, single-car household in Table 4.1.

The approach would be based on a categorisation of households by structure, and then the estimation of an average trip rate for each category of household for a specified set of journey purposes.

The statistical characteristics of this so-called 'category analysis' contrast strongly with those of regression-based approaches. The main advantage of category analysis is that it avoids some of the estimating problems, in particular, of non-linearity and multi-colinearity which appear to hamper regression analysis in this area. On the other hand, it is not always obvious in practice how much of the variation in observed trip-making between households is accounted for by the household classification adopted. In principle, however, it is possible to examine 'goodness of fit' in these circumstances using analysis of variance methods.

The form of category analysis currently used in much transportation planning work is based on the model developed by Wootton and Pick.[8] This used 108 possible household categories, made up of six household-structure types, six income classes and three car-ownership classes. The main criticisms that can be levelled at this approach is that it neglects a great deal of the information on the interrelationships of structure, income and car ownership of the kind discussed above. It also appears to neglect the evidence produced, for example, by Oi and Shuldiner on the independent influence of the income variable once car ownership and household structure have been standardised for. The evidence on this is shown in Table 4.2.[9]

TABLE 4.2

Household trip-generation rates for one car-owning household

Household size	Household income class		
	High	*Medium*	*Low*
1-person	1.41	1.20	0.99
2-person	2.79	2.72	2.70
3-person	3.74	2.98	3.28
4-person	4.05	3.81	3.94

Whilst trip-making increases monotonically with household size, the pattern with respect to household income is both weak and uneven. This suggests that it may be sufficient to use either a very coarse household-income grouping, or even to ignore income differences altogether in analysing trip-making. Taken together, these points suggest that the 108-category classification adopted is uneconomical in two respects. First, the household sample required is determined largely by the need to generate robust estimates of the mean values for each of the 108 categories. If households could be allocated to a smaller number of household categories by taking more account of interrelationships between classifying variables, then either sample size could be reduced, or more reliable estimates of the category means obtained. For example, if household income can be ignored once household structure and car ownership have been standardised for, then as few as eighteen household categories might be required. Second, the need to specify a joint distribution of households by income, structure, car ownership and zone of residence is likely to require an exceedingly complex and probably somewhat arbitrary forecasting process, with little check on potential biases.

Whichever approach to trip generation is adopted, a central element of the analysis and forecasting process is the estimation of future car-ownership levels. The previous discussion suggests that car ownership may be analysed as a function of income and structure, although it has usually been related both at the zonal and at the household level to household income and residential density. The approach has been to analyse differences in car ownership using a relationship of the following kind:

$$\log \left(\frac{P_0}{1 - P_0} \right) = a_0 + a_1 \log I + a_2 \log D, \qquad (4.3)$$

where P_0 = probability of a household being a zero-car-owning household; I = household or zonal average household income; and D = zonal residential density. The proportion of two or more car-owning households is then estimated as

$$\frac{P_2}{P_1} = b_0 + b_1 I + d_2 D. \qquad (4.4)$$

Because

$$P_0 + P_1 + P_2 = 1, \qquad (4.5)$$

1-car ownership is equal to $1 - P_0 - P_2$.

The major part of the variation between zonal average car-ownership levels is usually explained by the income variable.

Relationships of this kind have been found to give acceptably good fits when applied to cross-sectional data. Bates and Quarmby, however,[10] found that car-ownership levels were over-predicted when cross-section models were used to make backwards projections. One possible reason for this over-prediction is that variables which affect ownership are not included in cross-sectional analysis. The most likely omission here is the cost of car purchase and operation. As Tanner has shown,[11] this fell by almost 20 per cent in real terms over the period

used by Bates and Quarmby for back prediction. Car-ownership forecasts based on cross-sectional data now usually modify the forecast
growth rate of household incomes to take account of expected changes
in motoring costs, but this is a very crude procedure, and assumes that
the response to relative price changes is similar to the response to real
household-income changes.

Tanner's own work has analysed time-series data on car ownership
at an aggregative (national) level. The form of model used is based on a
logistic function whose upper limiting value is defined in terms of the
saturation car-ownership level. The basic form of model is one in which

$$\frac{dy}{dt} = ky\,(s - y), \tag{4.6}$$

where y = car-ownership level expressed as cars per person, s = saturation car-ownership level, and k = some function of average income per
person and car operating costs. Tanner suggests that

$$k = b_0 + b_1 \frac{1.dI}{I.dt} + b_2 \frac{1.dp}{P.dt}, \tag{4.7}$$

where I = average income per person, and P = an index of car-purchas-
ing and operating costs. In a forecasting context, the dominant influence
in this model is the level of saturation assumed. The speed at which car
ownership approaches this level is determined by k, which, in turn, in
Tanner's formulation, depends upon the forecast time paths of income
and car-operating costs, and the values of the income- and cost-
responsiveness parameters.

Because the model has only been estimated using national car-
ownership data and income, its applicability to local transport planning
is limited to providing an order-of-magnitude check on the car-ownership forecasts produced using local data. The most important limitation
of the Tanner model at a local level is that the saturation level of
ownership may well vary between one type of area and another —
depending, for example, on residential density and the quality of public-
transport services.

In principle, however, the time-series approach is strongly preferable
to the cross-sectional approach to car-ownership forecasting used in
most local studies. In particular, it is able to take explicit account of the
effects of car-purchase and operating cost changes on car-ownership
levels. In order to be operational at the local level, further analysis of
local saturation levels of car ownership is required. This, in conjunction

with work on restructuring the analysis of trip generation is an urgent research priority because the estimated benefits from longer-lived transport investment projects are often crucially dependent on the forecast trip volumes.

Trip Attractions and Non-Home 1-Based Journeys

The analysis of zonal trip attractions has received somewhat less attention than the analysis of trip generation. In general, the approach to trip attraction has been to explain the number of trips attracted to a zone for any specified journey purpose as a function of zonal land uses. For example, the number of work trips attracted is explained as a function of the number of employment opportunities, the number of education trips as a function of the number of school places, and the number of shopping trips as a function of retail employment.

Non-home based trips are usually analysed in the same way as trip attractions. They tend to be closely associated with certain land uses, such as offices, shops and institutions, and the propensity to generate trips is therefore analysed and forecast as a function of these land uses.

If the forecasting model used to distribute trips is of the doubly constrained kind, then consistency is required between the forecast numbers of trips generated and the forecast numbers of trip attractions summed over all zones. Because the forecast of trip generations is usually regarded as the best estimate of the total number of trips in the system, scaling factors are applied to zonal trip attractions in order to achieve the required consistency.

The Interaction Between Trip Generation and Attractionction and the and the Transport Network

A frequent criticism of the conventional approach to trip generation and attraction has been that it fails to allow for any interaction between the level of trip-making and the costs of travel. Empirical evidence on the significance of this is unfortunately sparse, but, *a priori*, two points can be made.

First, whilst in conventional trip-generation analysis, the total number of trips generated from a zone is not sensitive to the quality of the transport network, the number of *inter-zonal* trips is. In the conventional modelling process, the total number of trips made from a zone is the sum of intra-zonal trips plus inter-zonal trips. The costs of the intra-zonal trips are usually assumed not to alter when the inter-zonal network is changed. Thus, if the share of intra-zonal trips in total trip-making is a function of the relative costs of intra- and inter-zonal trips, changes in the quality of service offered by the network should affect this share.

Second, whilst conventional analysis has usually concentrated on the generation of vehicular trips, there is no reason in principle why work on trip generation should not also try to explain the number of walk and cycle trips made. Since walk and cycle trips may in some circumstances represent a serious alternative to vehicular trips, their neglect seems curious. According to the 1971 Census, 15 per cent of journeys to work were made on foot or by bicycle. In many smaller towns the walk/cycle share was considerably higher than this.

Some useful empirical evidence on the extent to which non-vehicular journeys appears in a paper by J. F. Kain.[12] The relevant empirical finding concerned the responsiveness of the proportion of a zone's population using a private car and public transport to changes in the quality of public-transport services. Very briefly, Kain found that at the sample means, a 1 per cent improvement in the quality of public-transport services would produce approximately an 0.3 per cent improvement in patronage. On the other hand, the improvement would reduce the proportion of workers using the private car by only 0.06 per cent. Since the percentage actually using the private car was about three times the percentage using public transport, the switch from private to public transport would represent a gain of about 0.18 per cent to public transport. This leaves about 0.12 per cent unaccounted for. Kain suggests that this balancing element represents switches from pedestrian or car passenger journeys. We may hypothesise that the major effect is a switch from pedestrian journeys.

This work is suggestive of the desirability of attempting to take some account of walk/cycle trips. If the total trip origins referred to both vehicular and non-vehicular trips, then a further possible margin of substitution would be offered in the modelling process. As with intra-zonal trips, it would be assumed that trip costs on non-vehicular mode were independent of the transport-network quality. Changes in the level of service on the network could then be reflected not only in shifts between inter- and intra-zonal trips, but also between non-vehicular and vehicular modes. A recent U.K. transportation study, carried out in Lincoln, calibrated a sequential set of models in which a walk/cycle mode is separately represented.[13]

This latter development in particular should go some way towards meeting the objection that conventional trip-generation procedures do not allow for interaction between level of service and vehicular trip-making. A potentially more serious difficulty, however, concerns the impact on zonal trip attractions of certain kinds of cost change which are highly specific to certain zones. The kind of cost change we are concerned with here is associated with the imposition of parking charges. The need to consider their impact arises in the context of examining alternative means of traffic restraint. Relatively high parking charges may be used in this context as a means of controlling the number of private vehicle trips in certain parts of an urban centre. Parking charges may alter the relative costs of different destinations more than other kinds of transport network change. Predicting their impact may therefore be seen as one aspect of a much wider problem concerning the use of models to predict outcomes outside the range of values of the variables with which they have been estimated.

We might expect that the responsiveness of total vehicular trip destinations in a particular zone to changes of this kind would be a function of the availability of alternative trip-end opportunities for the journey purpose in question. For some purposes, such as work or employers' business, the degree of sensitivity may be negligible. For other purposes, such as shopping, where a wider choice of alternative destinations exists, the imposition of high parking charges in particular zones might be expected to have some effect on the total number of trip ends.

In conclusion we may say that there is little or no empirical evidence on the responsiveness of total trip-making (vehicular and non-vehicular) to network level of service. *A priori* we might expect that whilst the level of vehicular trip-making may show some sensitivity, it is less obvious that total trip-making will be similarly responsive. If this is the case then the inclusion of a non-vehicular mode in the modelling process may go some way to meeting the criticisms that have been made about the absence of interaction between trip generation and attraction and transport costs.

CHAPTER FIVE

A Digression - The Specification of Travel Costs in the Analysis of Travel Demand

The main purpose of this chapter is to discuss the concept of the 'generalised cost of travel', which has been extensively used in the analysis and forecasting of travel-demand and transport networks. The treatment is introductory in some respects, and certain problems which arise in the specification of generalised cost are discussed elsewhere in the book, notably in the chapters on modal choice and evaluation.

Travel by vehicular modes involves the user in at least two different types of expenditure – the money outlays involved in ticket purchase, for example, and the expenditure of time taken up in travelling. In some situations these two outlays may be quite highly correlated, and perhaps for this reason early North American work on transport planning used only travel time as a proxy for 'cost'. The inadequacy of this treatment became apparent as demand analysis became increasingly concerned with problems of choice between different modes of travel, each of which might display very different travel time – out-of-pocket cost relationships. In addition to this, there are elements of travel cost, parking charges in particular, whose incidence on trip cost are entirely independent of trip length.

The approach which has been used in the sequential modelling procedure has been to express the different outlays in terms of a single unit. This involves the conversion of units of time into money units or vice versa, and hence the use of an exchange rate between the two types of outlay.

The possibility of estimating people's value of time in the context of decisions about travel rests on the existence of situations in which they can make trade-offs between time and money outlays on travel. Harrison and Quarmby list a number of situations where this kind of trade-off can be examined:[1]

(1) choice of destination;
(2) choice of travel mode;
(3) choice of route;
(4) choice of speed at which to drive; and

(5) choice of relative location of home and work.

In the case of mode choice, people may have the opportunity of travelling either on mode A or mode B. Travel on mode A involves higher out-of-pocket expenses, but smaller travel times. The methodology by which values of time are derived from observations of people's choices in these circumstances has been extensively described elsewhere.[2] We therefore content ourselves with extracting the results which are most relevant to travel-demand analysis and forecasting. These are as follows.

(1) It is necessary to distinguish between different elements of journey time since their perceived disutilities (and hence their valuation) are not equal. The three elements usually distinguished for vehicular journeys are the following.

(a) *Walk or access time*. This is the time spent walking from or to the ultimate trip origin or destinations to or from the beginning and end points of the vehicular stage of the journey. As indicated in Chapter 3, the network descriptions used in transport modelling include 'connectors' between the zone centroid and the points of access to the transport network. In the case of public-transport networks these access points represent bus stops or stations, and the 'cost' associated with the connector' link therefore embodies an estimate of the average time taken to walk from a trip origin to an access point.

(b) *Waiting time*. This is self-explanatory and is associated only with public-transport travel modes. The network description will include an estimate of the average waiting time for each access point on the network. In the case of non-scheduled or frequent services, the waiting time is usually estimated as half the average vehicle headways, on the assumption that passenger arrivals at the access point are random. For scheduled services, however, it is assumed that the arrival times are more closely tied to the schedule. The average waiting time for scheduled services is therefore assumed to be considerably less than for unscheduled services for any given level of service frequency.

(c) *In-vehicle time*. Early mode-choice studies which did not distinguish between walk/access time and waiting time gave the combined out-of-vehicle time elements a weighting approximately two to three times as high as in-vehicle time. Goldberg has suggested that walk/access time involves somewhat less disutility than waiting time and this result does accord with *a priori* expectations.[3] Current U.K. practice is to use a weighting of unity for in-vehicle time and two for all out-of-vehicle time.[4]

(2) The value of units of in-vehicle time is estimated to be about 20-30 per cent of personal income per unit of time. Two obvious implications of this 'proportionality' result are, first, that it suggests the need for a set of income-specific generalised cost matrices, and, second, that the value of time increases over time as average incomes increase. Hence, *ceteris paritas*, the time elements in any generalised cost expression will increase in importance relative to the money-outlay elements. The 'simple proportionality' result has been challenged, for example, in work by the Local Government Operational Research Unit,[5] which has claimed not to find any strong relationship between value of time and income. Practical work in the context of urban transportation studies has not generally attempted to construct disaggregated cost matrices, at least below the level of disaggregation of car-owning and non-car-owning households.

(3) A distinction has been drawn in the evaluation context between travel time which takes place in the course of work, and travel time occurring during leisure time. In-work travel time has generally been valued for evaluation purposes at the wage rate plus labour-on costs, on the assumption that this represents the value of an employee's time to an employer. The resulting value of time is therefore considerably higher than the leisure time value. However, it is not obvious that this higher value is relevant to people's behavioural choices. Current practice on the extent to which in-work time is taken account of in the construction of cost matrices varies considerably. In the absence of any firm empirical evidence on the point, there is much to be said for an uncomplicated approach to these matters. This would support the use of a single behavioural cost matrix for all journey purposes.

(4) An important result of work on mode choice which is only indirectly related to the value of time concerns the extent to which the marginal costs of car use are perceived by car users. The full marginal cost of car use includes mileage-related depreciation and maintenance costs, as well as fuel costs. Quarmby's work suggested that the perceived costs of car use, in the sense of the cost which best explained people's observed choice of mode, might only be about 50 per cent of the full marginal cost.[6] He observed that this perceived cost was close to the estimated marginal fuel cost. Subsequent work has indicated that perceived motoring costs may be even less than the ones estimated by Quarmby.[7] There has been some speculation on whether this might reflect the extent to which private motoring is subsidised by employers. This divergence between perceived and full marginal costs creates

certain difficulties in the context of evaluation. In the present demand-forecasting and analysis context, however, it is necessary only to note that the 'perceived costs on which people appear to base their travel decisions are less than full marginal costs and to incorporate the relevant perceived costs in network descriptions.

Generalised Cost and Generalised Time

The generalised cost of travel from i to j by mode K and for a person in the nth income group can be written in one of two equivalent ways:

$$^{c}c_{ijk}^{n} = p_{ijk} + v_{iv}^{n} t_{ijk}^{iv} + v_{a}^{n} t_{ijk}^{a} + v_{w}^{n} t_{ijk}^{w} \tag{5.1}$$

or

$$^{t}c_{ijk}^{n} = \frac{^{c}c_{ijk}^{n}}{v_{iv}^{n}} = \frac{p_{ijk}}{v_{iv}^{n}} + t_{ijk}^{iv} + a_{1}t_{ijk}^{a} + a_{2}t_{ijk}^{w}, \tag{5.2}$$

where $^{c}c_{ijk}^{n}$ = generalised cost in money units, $^{t}c_{ijk}^{n}$ = generalised cost in time units, p_{ijk} = ijk out-of-pocket expenses, t_{ijk}^{iv} = ijk in-vehicle time, t_{ijk}^{a} = ijk access time, t_{ijk}^{w} = ijk wait time, v_{iv}^{n} = value of in-vehicle time for nth income group, v_{a}^{n} = value of access time for nth income group, v_{w}^{n} = value of wait time for nth income group, and $a_{1,2}$ = v_{aw}^{n}/v_{iv}^{n}.

Writing the generalised cost in these two equivalent forms points up a potential source of difficulty. If the value of time is an increasing function of income, and if average incomes are expected to increase through time, then

(*a*) generalised cost in money units (with p_{ijk} constant) increases through time, but

(*b*) generalised cost in time units (with p_{ijk} constant) declines.

As Goodwin has pointed out,[8] there has been very little published discussion of the case for using one sort of cost rather than another for forecasting purposes. Two arguments have been advanced, however, for the use of time units rather than cost units. The first, advanced by McIntosh and Quarmby,[9] is that it is more plausible to assume a constant marginal utility of time than a constant marginal utility of income. Hence, assuming a diminishing marginal utility of income, 'as incomes rise, so a given (money) cost will carry less weight'. The second argument, put forward by Wagon and Wilson is that if generalised costs are expressed in money units, then, *ceteris paribus*, the average trip lengths forecast by certain conventional models (of the sequential kind) will decrease through time.[10] This they feel is intuitively implausible. It can in fact be shown that this outcome results from an incorrect application of the model in question. If the model is correctly applied, then the forecasts it produces are independent of the choice of cost units.

Underlying both of these arguments may be an awareness that the form of model used to distribute trips in the conventional sequential structure does not directly incorporate any equivalent of the 'income elasticity of demand' concept. It may therefore be thought that changes in income should somehow be taken account of by changing generalised costs. However, it can be shown that the effects of changing income levels can be incorporated directly into the distribution/modal-split model; this is discussed in more detail in the next chapter. If this is the case then the first argument is also somewhat weakened.

There remains the problem of whether the generalised cost concept developed above can be appropriately used in the single-stage model of the kind discussed in Chapter 3. It will be remembered that a model of this kind takes the following form:

$$t_{ijk} = a_0 L_i^{a_1} L_j^{a_2} C_{ijk}^{a_3} C_{ijm}^{a_4}, \tag{5.3}$$

where t_{ijk} = ijk trips, $L_{i,j}$ = land-use variables, $C_{ijk,m}$ = travel costs by modes k, m, and $a_0 - a_4$ = empirically derived coefficients.

If C_{ijk} and C_{ijm} are expressed in conventional generalised cost terms, then the volume of ijk trips will alter over time even in the absence of any land-use changes, or changes in network performance. Moreover, the direction of change will depend upon the choice of units. Clearly this dependence on the choice of units is unsatisfactory. The answer is that the application of a generalised cost expression of the kind derived above is not appropriate for models of this kind. Instead, as in the Domencich – Kraft - Valette example discussed in Chapter 3,[11] it is necessary to estimate the model using not generalised cost values of time applied to the time components, but simply the time components themselves. That is to say, the estimating equation takes the following form:

$$t_{ijk} = a_0 L_i^{a_1} L_j^{a_2} P_{ijk}^{a_3} t_{ijk}^{a_4} P_{ijm}^{a_5} t_{ijm}^{a_6}, \tag{5.4}$$

where $P_{ijk,m}$ = ijk,m out-of-pocket cost, and $t_{ijk,m}$ = ijk,m travel time.

For forecasting purposes, the coefficients $a_3 - a_6$ would then be used in conjunction with the forecast values of out-of-pocket costs and travel times.

CHAPTER SIX

Trip Distribution

Introduction

The analysis and forecasting of the areal distribution of journeys usually forms the second stage in the sequential process set out in Chapter 3. Methods of forecasting trip distribution have varied considerably, both in complexity and in the nature of the assumptions which are made about the factors affecting travel patterns. The first part of the chapter briefly examines the growth-factor approach in which the forecast trip distribution is independent of transport-network factors. The remaining sections discuss models whose forecasts are sensitive both to land-use and transport-network factors.

Growth-Factor Forecasting Methods

This form of forecasting 'model' is based on the application of growth factors reflecting land-use changes to existing levels of inter-zonal trip-making. The very simplest form of growth-factor procedure, which was used in some early U.S. studies, is to factor up the existing matrix of $i-j$ traffic flows by a uniform factor which would reflect forecast changes in population, employment or car ownership for the area as a whole. The assumption of a uniform rate of increase for all inter-zonal flows is of course a highly restrictive one. In practice, the rate of growth of trip attraction and generation may vary quite widely between zones, and inter-zonal movements are therefore unlikely to grow at a uniform rate. This point may be illustrated by a numerical example. Consider an area consisting of three zones, A, B and C. Ignoring intra-zonal trip-making, the total number of trips 'destinating' in zone A, D_A will be equal to

$$T_{CA} + T_{BA} = D_A.$$

The current observed values of the flows T_{CA} and T_{BA} are 100 and 200 respectively, and D_A is therefore equal to 300. From the trip-generation stage, the forecast volume of journeys generated in the whole area is expected to increase by 50 per cent. However, the volume of trips attracted to A is forecast to increase by only 20 per cent. Application of the area-wide growth factor to the CA and BA flows would then produce a forecast of trip destinations in A of 450, whilst forecast trip attractions would only be 360. Achieving consistency between the sum of T_{CA} and T_{BA} and the exogenously forecast D_A therefore requires iteration, for example by applying a factor of

$$\frac{D_A^*}{T_{CA}^0 + T_{BA}^0},$$

where D_A^* = the exogenously given forecast of trip attraction to A, and T_{CA}^0, T_{BA}^0 = flows forecast by applying a uniform growth factor to each of the flows into A. There are a variety of iteration methods available for achieving a satisfactory balance between the sums of the flow figures and the exogenously given row and column sum totals of the trip matrix.[1] The criterion for choosing between them has generally been based on the rapidity with which convergence is achieved.

The effectiveness of even the more sophisticated growth-factor methods is likely to be limited in areas which are rapidly expanding or are experiencing changes in the pattern of land use. No doubt it is possible to make *ad hoc* adjustments to forecasting procedures to take account of these factors in a rough and ready way. Nevertheless, the conventional wisdom has been that growth-factor methods should only be used for relatively short-term forecasting in situations where population and land-use patterns are stable.

Perhaps the most important characteristic of growth-factor methods is that the changes in person journey flows which they predict are entirely independent of changes in the transport network. No attempt is made to 'explain' the pattern of flows in terms of an interaction between land use and transport. The existing pattern is, quite simply, whatever it is. Models of this kind therefore embody an extreme hypothesis about the sensitivity of travel patterns to transport-network changes. Subsequent developments in the analysis and forecasting of travel demand, however, have attempted to analyse current patterns of trip distribution in terms both of land-use and transport-network factors.

Analytical Models of Trip Distribution

The remainder of the chapter describes models whose forecasts are sensitive to both land-use and transport-network factors. Three forms of model can be distinguished:

 (1) unconstrained models;

(2) singly constrained models; and
(3) doubly constrained models.

The constraints relate to the row and column sum totals of the trip-making matrix, and the extent to which these are allowed to vary in response to changes in transport-network costs.

The unconstrained and singly constrained forms are straightforward demand models. The doubly constrained model is somewhat different; it is based on the recognition that under certain circumstances, trip-makers may be competing for a given number of trip-end opportunities.

(1) Unconstrained Models

In the unconstrained model the total number of trips originating or destinating in a zone is allowed to vary freely with changes in transport-network costs. An example of this form of model is the single-stage model introduced in Chapter 3. The usual way of estimating models of this kind is regression, in which the dependent variable is the volume of $i-j$ trips (often by mode k). The explanatory variables are land-use factors in the origin and destination zones, and travel costs. The general form of the model introduced in Chapter 3 was as follows:[2]

$$T_{ijk} = f(G_i, A_j, C_{ijk}, C_{ijm}, t_{ijk}, t_{ijm}), \qquad (6.1)$$

where T_{ijk} = $i-j$ trips by mode k, G_i = land-use factors in the origin zone, A_j, = land-use factors in the destination zone, C_{ijk} = $i-j$ travel cost by mode k, C_{ijm} = $i-j$ travel cost by mode m, t_{ijk} = $i-j$ travel time by mode k, and t_{ijm} = $i-j$ travel time by mode m.

(2) Singly Constrained Models

In the singly constrained model either the column (trip destination) or, more usually, the row (trip origin) sums are constant. In the latter case, therefore, the total number of trips generated from a zone is predetermined at the trip-generation stage. The distribution model then distributes these trips as a function of travel cost and the relative strengths of the attraction in the destination zones. In order for the row sums to be equal to O_i, the model takes the following form:

$$T_{ij} = O_i \left\{ D_j f(C_{ij}) \left(\sum_j D_j f(C_{ij}) \right)^{-1} \right. \qquad (6.2)$$

$$= O_i A_i D_j f(C_{ij}), \qquad (6.3)$$

where $A_i = \Sigma_j D_j f(C_{ij})^{-1}$. Here, D_j is some measure of attractiveness of zone j, such as employment or retail floor-space. A_i is then a balancing factor to ensure that $\Sigma_j T_{ij} = O_i$.

(3) Doubly Constrained Models

In the doubly constrained models, balancing factors are applied both in respect of trip origins and trip destinations. This ensures that, to some acceptable degree of accuracy, constraints are satisfied in respect of both row and column sum totals. Thus

$$\sum_j T_{ij} = O_i \text{ and } \sum_i T_{ij} = D_j,$$

and the model takes the form

$$T_{ij} = O_i A_i D_j B_j f(C_{ij}), \tag{6.4}$$

where $B_j = \Sigma_i \left\{ O_i A_i f(C_{ij}) \right\}^{-1}$. Satisfaction of the two sets of constraints cannot be achieved simultaneously. The model is therefore iterated, rather in the fashion of the growth-factor methods, so that having initially applied the row sum constraints, each column sum is factored by an amount equal to D_j/D_j^* where D_j is the 'correct' column sum and D_j^* the column sum produced by applying the row sum constraint. The row sum figures would then, in turn, be adjusted by factors O_i/O_i^*.

The Significance of Trip-End Constraints

In both the unconstrained and singly constrained models, trip-making patterns are explained in terms of 'demand-side' factors only. Trips between i and j are determined by the land-use characteristics of i and j and the transport costs between them. The unconstrained, or single-stage model, takes no explicit account of the competition provided by zones other than j_i. The singly constrained model views the trip-maker as choosing from a set of alternative destination zones. However, the choice of destination zone is not constrained in any way by the choices of trip-makers in other origin zones.

The doubly constrained model, on the other hand, recognises that under certain circumstances trip-makers may be competing for a limited number of trip-end opportunities in any specific zone. If the total number of trip-end opportunities in a zone is exogenously determined, then the application of a singly constrained (or unconstrained) model may result in a prediction that more or less trips than the exogenously given total will destinate there. In principle it might be argued that the constraint should be in the form of 'less than or equal to', rather than 'equal to'. However, this may produce inconsistencies at an aggregate level. For example, the total number of school trips predicted may be less than the number of schoolchildren.

Apart from education trips, the most obvious journey purpose to which the doubly constrained form of model applies is work journeys. In the short term at least, the number of zonal employment opportunities may be assumed to be independent of transport-network factors (at the local level), and so people's choices of destination for the work trips are no longer independent of those of other people. The exact mechanism through which the trip-end constraint is made effective need not be specified. Two obvious alternative extreme hypotheses are, first, that wage rates in zones of relatively high accessibility are bid down so that, given the levels of transport costs prevailing, demand and supply are brought into equilibrium; second, that employers in zones of relatively low accessibility have to bid up wages to attract labour. We might further hypothesise that the relative strength of these two effects will be a function of the over-all tightness of labour markets.

It is sometimes suggested that the imposition of trip-end constraints at the destination end is synonymous with that constancy of land use which transport demand models assume. This is too restrictive a view however. It can be accepted that for journey-to-work and education trips, the land-use variables, employment opportunities and education places, respectively, are closely related to expected trip-end totals. For other types of trip, however, the relevant land-use variable may not bear anything like a fixed relationship with trip ends. For shopping trips, for example, land use, as measured by retail floor-space, may remain constant, although the predicted trip attraction may alter as a result of transport-network changes.

Finally, differences in the extent to which the trip-distribution model is constrained have some consequences for the predicted responsiveness of trip-making patterns to changes in transport-network costs. This can be illustrated by examining the own travel cost elasticity, defined as $(\partial T_{ij}/\partial C_{ij})$ (C_{ij}/T_{ij}), of i–j trip-making under the three alternative types of constraint. We assume in each case that the deterrence (or trip-cost) function is of the form C_{ij}^a (with $a < 0$).

In the unconstrained case, where the demand function may take the form

$$T_{ij} = a_0 G_i^{a_1} D_j^{a_2} C_{ij}^{a_3}, \tag{6.5}$$

the own cost elasticity of $i-j$ trip-making is equal to a_3.

In the singly (origin) constrained case the demand function takes the form

$$T_{ij} = O_i \frac{D_j C_{ij}^{a_3}}{\sum_j D_j C_{ij}^{a_3}}, \tag{6.6}$$

noting that

$$\log T_{ij} = \log O_i + \log D_j + a_3 \log C_{ij} - \log \sum_j (D_j C_{ij}^{a_3}) \tag{6.7}$$

$$\frac{C_{ij}}{T_{ij}} \frac{\partial T_{ij}}{\partial C_{ij}} = a_3 \left(1 - \frac{D_j C_{ij}^a}{\sum_j D_j C_{ij}^{a_3}}\right) = a_3 (1 - S_{ij}^i). \tag{6.8}$$

Thus elasticity is inversely related to the market share of trips from i taken by $i-j$ trips, S_{ij}^i. As market share tends to zero, elasticity tends to a_3; as market share approaches unity, elasticity tends to zero.

It is not possible to derive an equivalent elasticity expression for the doubly constrained case. But it can be seen intuitively that the absolute value of the elasticity coefficient will certainly be no greater than in the singly constrained case. Under (6.6) above, total trip attractions to j will increase as C_{ij} declines, since a change in $i-j$ trip patterns does not affect the volume of trip-making from other zones to j. Application of the destination-end constraints will then reduce the total number of trip attractions from each origin zone (including the ith) so as to satisfy the exogenously given trip-end constraint for j.

In the unconstrained case, the estimated coefficient with respect to the cost of travel influences both the market share of i trips held by the $i-j$ pair, and the total number of trips from i. Thus

$$\frac{dO_i}{dC_{ij}} = \frac{dT_{ij}}{dC_{ij}}. \tag{6.9}$$

In both the singly and doubly constrained cases dO_i/dC_{ij} is equal to zero. An alternative approach which would be intermediate between these two extreme assumptions about the relationship between O_i and C_{ij} would be a model of the following form:

$$T_{ij} = g \left(\sum_j C_{ij} \right) \left\{ D_j f(C_{ij}) \right\} \left\{ \sum_j D_j f(C_{ij}) \right\}^{-1}, \qquad (6.10)$$

where $g'(\Sigma_j C_{ij}) < 0$. This takes us back to the problem identified in the last section of Chapter 3, on trip generation and attraction — that of estimating a relationship between a zone's general accessibility and the total level of trip-making from it. Until more is known about this, and about the extent to which the inclusion of non-vehicular modes in the model takes care of it, the choice between alternative specifications has to be made on *a priori* grounds. Current practice is firmly based on the constrained approach.

Model Estimation

The estimation of the unconstrained distribution model by multiple regression poses no particular problems other than those such as multi-collinearity or the specification (linear, log linear, and so on) of the estimating equation. Coefficients are estimated in respect of both land-use factors at origin and estimation zones and transport-network factors, and there is no *a priori* constraint imposed on the size of these coefficients.

The singly constrained model may also be estimated using regression or maximum likelihood methods in the following way. We note first that

$$T_{ij} = O_i f(D_j, C_{ij}) \sum_j f(D_j, C_{ij})^{-1}. \qquad (6.11)$$

Because the term

$$\sum_j f(D_j, C_{ij})$$

is the same for all j, we may write

$$\frac{T_{ij}}{T_{ik}} = \frac{f(D_j, C_{ij})}{f(D_k, C_{ik})} \text{ for all } i. \qquad (6.12)$$

The singly constrained model may then be estimated as a form of market-shares model. For example, if

$$f(D_j, C_{ij}) = D_j^{b_1} e^{b_2 C_{ij}},$$

then the estimating equation would be

$$\log T_{ij} - \log T_{ik} = b_0 + b_1 (\log D_j - \log D_k) + b_2 (C_{ij} - C_{ik}),$$
(6.13)

with b_0 constrained to equal 0. In this formulation b_1 may be interpreted as a 'scale effect'. The size of b_2 then indicates the slope of what may be called the 'deterrence function'; the larger the value of b_2, the stronger the deterrent effects of travel costs.[3] *A priori*, we would expect this to vary systematically between journey purposes. Since the market shares estimated in this way may not sum to unity, it may be necessary to apply an appropriate scaling factor to the estimates.

The earlier discussion of the doubly constrained model assumed implicitly (in equation (6.4), for example) that the measure of 'attractiveness' at zone j, D_j, was in fact equal to the number of trip ends in zone j. In the following section we shall see that if the model is interpreted in a probability-maximising sense, then this constraint on both trip origins and destinations is necessary. In this case, the estimation of the doubly constrained model involves a search for a value of the coefficients b_2 which satisfies the exogenously given constraints.

However, it is also possible to impose a destination trip-end constraint on a model which may initially be estimated in the manner of equation (6.13) above. In this equation, the term D_j refers to whatever measure (or combination of measures) of attractiveness is the most appropriate for the trip purpose in question. If a constraint is imposed on the number of trips destinating at j (of the form $\Sigma_i T_{ij} = E_j$, where E_j refers to the number of 'permitted' trip ends at j) the balancing factor B_j has to be slightly differently specified to the B_j in equation (6.4). Then it was equal simply to $\Sigma_i \{O_i A_i f(C_{ij})\}^{-1}$. If D_j is no longer equal to E_j, B_j must now be expressed as $E_j [\Sigma_i O_i A_i f(D_j, C_{ij})]^{-1}$.

The Alternative Foundations of Trip-Distribution Models and their Implications for Forecasting

The discussion so far has been concerned with models of trip distribution which seek to explain travel behaviour at a point in time and then to use the estimated coefficients in conjunction with forecast values of the relevant explanatory variables to produce forecasts of trip distribution. We now turn to an alternative approach to the distribution model based on an explicit probability-maximising approach.[4] Although this bears a superficial resemblance to the kind of model described earlier, it does differ fundamentally in the way in which it is used for forecasting.

The probability-maximising model defines that distribution of trips which is the most likely given certain constraints. These constraints relate first to trip ends and are identical to those represented in the discussion of doubly constrained models above:

$$\sum_j T_{ij} = O_i \text{ and } \sum_i T_{ij} = D_j. \tag{6.14}$$

Second, a constraint is imposed on the total expenditure on travel so that

$$E = \sum_i \sum_j T_{ij} C_{ij}. \tag{6.15}$$

The number of possible 'states of the world', in relation to which the most probable distribution is to be defined, is given in terms of the number of possible trip configurations which satisfy both the trip-end and expenditure constraints. A single trip configuration is given by the number of ways in which a set of individual trip-makers can behave in such a way as to generate a specified trip pattern. If the total number of trip-makers (and trips in the system) is T, then this is equal to

$$\frac{T!}{(T - T_{11})! \, T_{11}!} \times \frac{(T - T_{11})!}{T_{12}!(T - T_{11} - T_{12})!} = \frac{T!}{T \, \frac{\pi}{ij}} \tag{6.16}$$

If this is defined as $e(T_{ij})$, then the number of possible states of the world is $\Sigma e(T_{ij})$, where the summation is over all configurations which satisfy the constraint equations. The most probable distribution is then that which maximises the function $\Sigma e(T_{ij})$ subject to the constraints. The solution of this constrained maximisation problem makes use of the result that

$$\log X! = X \log X - \log X. \tag{6.17}$$

Thus, we wish to maximise the function

$$L = \log \Sigma \, e(T_{ij}) + \sum_i \lambda_i^1 (O_i - \sum_j T_{ij}) + \sum_j \lambda_j^2 (D_j - \sum_i T_{ij})$$

$$+ b \, (E - \sum_i \sum_j T_{ij} \, C_{ij}). \tag{6.18}$$

Differentiating (6.18) with respect to T_{ij} and using (6.17) we obtain

$$\frac{\partial L}{\partial T_{ij}} = - \log T_{ij} - \lambda_i^1 - \lambda_j^2 - bc_{ij}. \tag{6.19}$$

At a maximum, $\partial L/(\partial T_{ij}) = 0$ so that

$$T_{ij} = e^{-\lambda_i^1 - \lambda_j^2 - bc_{ij}}. \tag{6.20}$$

This can be transformed into the more familiar form of a doubly constrained model. Since

$$\sum_j T_{ij} = O_i e^{-\lambda_i^1} \; (\sum_j e^{-\lambda_j^2 - bc_{ij}}) \tag{6.21}$$

$$e^{-\lambda_i^1} = O_i \; (\sum_j e^{-\lambda_j^2 - bc_{ij}})^{-1} \tag{6.22}$$

Let

$$A_i = \frac{e^{-\lambda_i^1}}{O_i}.$$

Similarly, let

$$B_j = \frac{e^{-\lambda_j^2}}{D_j}.$$

Hence, substituting in (6.20)

$$T_{ij} = O_i A_i D_j B_j e^{-bc_{ij}}. \tag{6.23}$$

The form of the deterrence function in (6.20) is of course determined by the form of the expenditure constraint. If, for example, the constraint had been written as

$$\sum_i \sum_j T_{ij} \log C_{ij} = E, \tag{6.24}$$

then the expression for T_{ij} would have been

$$T_{ij} = O_i A_i D_j B_j C_{ij}^{-b}. \tag{6.25}$$

Alternatively, the expenditure constraints could be specified as a composite of the absolute and logged forms, such as

$$\sum_i \sum_j T_{ij} \log C_{ij} + \sum_i \sum_j T_{ij} C_{ij} = E, \tag{6.26}$$

in which case the expression for T_{ij} would have been

$$T_{ij} = O_i A_i D_j B_j C_{ij}^{-b_1} e^{-b_2 C_{ij}}. \qquad (6.27)$$

The significance of the form in which the expenditure constraint is specified is that it embodies people's perception of the deterrent effects of travel costs. Wilson has suggested that 'in study areas where trip costs are generally small (such as urban studies) the negative exponential function is likely to fit best, while in study areas where trip costs are larger, for example inter-urban studies, the power function is likely to fit best'.[5]

The important point to notice here is that the empirical content of the probability-maximising approach only enters through the specification of the constraint equations. In strong contrast to the 'behavioural' approach, the probability-maximising approach requires the calibration of a model based on observed trip-making data only in order to test alternative specifications of the expenditure constraint.

The use of the probability-maximising model for forecasting purposes is thus fundamentally different from the behavioural model which seeks to 'explain' an observed pattern of behaviour and then to forecast using the estimated coefficients in conjunction with forecasts of the relevant explanatory variables. Thus, in the singly constrained case,

$$T_{ij}^F = O_i^F f(D_j^F, C_{ij}^F) \ (\sum_j f(D_j^F, C_{ij}^F)^{-1}), \qquad (6.28)$$

where the F superscripts represent forecast values, and the function, $f(D_j, C_{ij})$ is estimated using observed travel-survey data. The total level of expenditure travel is an output of the modelling process. By contrast, the total expenditure on travel is an input to the forecasting process using the probability-maximising procedure. Furthermore, although the form of the deterrence function is derived from a calibration on observed travel-survey data, the parameters of the function are themselves outputs of the forecasting procedure.

The potential significance of this difference in approach is difficult to judge since no tests have been done to compare the forecasts produced by the two processes. Indeed, so far as one is aware, no attempt has been made to forecast using the probability-maximising approach. Wilson's empirical work in the field, embodied in the SELNEC transportation study,[6] has been based on a behavioural approach.

In the absence of available empirical evidence, we simply make four *a priori* points about the potential utility of these alternative approaches to forecasting.

First, very little work has been done on forecasting expenditure on person journeys, which is required as an input to the probability-maximising approach. What work there has been has related consumers' expenditure on travel (often including car purchase) to incomes. But little is known about the over-all price elasticity of demand and hence the way in which total expenditure might alter in response to policies which have a significant effect on the cost of travel. Moreover, the notion of 'generalised cost', which is generally considered to be appropriate in this context, embodies both time and money outlays. Whilst some work is now being done on time budgets,[7] it is still at an early stage, and little is known about how time budgets alter over time. There are therefore real difficulties to be overcome before progress can be made with the probability-maximising approach. However, it is also surely true that the forecast levels of expenditure on trip-making which 'emerge' from the behavioural models should be closely examined to see if the expenditure elasticities which they imply are consistent with *a priori* expectations. Beesley's comments on the original London Transportation Study are very relevant here.[8]

Second, as we shall see in the following chapter on modal choice, the probability-maximising approach to forecasting encounters certain difficulties in combining the representation of mode choice and trip-distribution behaviour.

Third, although the earlier discussion of constraints suggested the desirability of using a singly rather than a double constrained form of model for journey purposes other than work and education, it is not easy to see how the probability-maximising model can be used in anything other than a doubly constrained manner. If the destination-end constraint is omitted, trips are distributed on the basis of the relative size of the deterrence function, so

$$T_{ij} = O_i A_i e^{-bc_{ij}}, \tag{6.29}$$

where $A_i = (\Sigma_j e^{-bc_{ij}})^{-1}$. Only if some means can be found of relating changes in D_j to zonal accessibility, so that D_j in the doubly constrained model becomes variable with respect to transport-network characteristics, can this lack of flexibility be overcome.

Finally, the probability-maximising approach does overcome some of the problems of travel-cost specification which may arise with behavioural models. We now turn to this topic.

The Specification of Generalised Cost in Trip-Distribution Forecasting

Chapter 5 discussed certain problems in applying the concept of 'generalised cost'. We now develop this discussion in the context of trip distribution, examining first the appropriate specification of generalised cost for forecasting with a behavioural model, and, second, in the probability-maximising approach.

It was suggested towards the end of Chapter 5 that a composite expression of the kind

$$c_{ij} = m_{ij} + vt_{ij}, \qquad (6.30)$$

where $c_{ij} = i-j$ generalised cost, $m_{ij} = i-j$ out-of-pocket cost, $t_{ij} = i-j$ travel time, and v = value of time, was inappropriate for use in an unconstrained model if v was assumed to be time-dependent. Exactly the same conclusion applies to the singly (and doubly) constrained behavioural models. If a composite generalised cost expression in which v is time-dependent is used in conjunction with an estimated deterrence function, then the forecast trip distribution will vary with the choice of units for c_{ij}. If c_{ij} is expressed in money units (as in (6.21) above) then, with $dv/dt > 0$, the average trip length will tend to shorten. Conversely, if c_{ij} is expressed in time units, then, with $dv/dt > 0$, the average trip length will tend to lengthen.

As reported in Chapter 5, the use of generalised cost in time units has sometimes been recommended for forecasting trip distribution on the grounds that it may import an 'income effect' into the model which is not explicitly allowed for in any other way. This argument is not obviously convincing, for at least three reasons. First, income effects are already allowed for explicitly in the over-all forecasting process at the trip-generation stage. Second, increasing car ownership and use which is embodied in the forecasting procedure reflects a preference for faster, but also longer-distance travel, which is income related. Finally, income effects can be allowed for explicitly at the distribution stage through disaggregation of the trip-distribution model by income groups.

As was indicated in Chapter 5, the simultaneous effects of travel time and money outlays can only be satisfactorily incorporated in the forecasting process using behavioural models through the separate specification of deterrence function with respect to each factor. The singly constrained model would then be specified as

$$T_{ij} = O_i f(D_j, m_{ij}, t_{ij}) \sum_j f(D_{j'}, m_{ij}, t_{ij}). \qquad (6.31)$$

In this form, the forecast trip distribution would be independent of choice of units.

The forecasts produced by the probability-maximising model are also independent of the choice of generalised cost units. If money units are used, then the total expenditure constraint takes the following form:

$$E^M = \sum_i \sum_j T_{ij} (m_{ij} + vt_{ij}). \qquad (6.32)$$

If generalised time units are used, then the constraint is written as

$$E^T = \sum_i \sum_j T_{ij} \left(\frac{m_{ij}}{v} + t_{ij} \right) = \frac{E^M}{V}. \qquad (6.33)$$

It follows that since $T_{ij}^M = T_{ij}^T$, that is the $i-j$ trip volumes are independent of choice of units, the relationship between the coefficients of the deterrence function is that

$$b^m = \frac{b^T}{v}. \qquad (6.34)$$

Moreover, it can be argued that any form of generalised cost function imports certain assumptions into the modelling process about the trade-off between time and money expenditure. A more fundamental approach which avoids the need to incorporate an exogenously given value of time is to disaggregate the expenditure constraint into time and money elements. Instead of a single constraint, therefore, we would have

$$E_1 = \sum_i \sum_j T_{ij} m_{ij} \qquad (6.35)$$

and

$$E_2 = \sum_i \sum_j T_{ij} t_{ij}.$$

The expression for T_{ij} would then have separate terms reflecting the time and cost constraints; thus

$$T_{ij} = O_i A_i D_j B_j e^{-b_1 m_{ij}} e^{-b_2 t_{ij}}. \qquad (6.36)$$

In this form the treatment parallels that embodied in the singly constrained behavioural model described in equation (6.29) above.

Finally, it should be noted that the probability-maximising approach can readily accommodate disaggregation by person type or income group and can embody expenditure constraints which are income-group specific. Trip-end constraints may be specified for person type n, at least at the trip origin end as follows:

$$\sum_j T_{ij}^n = O_i^n \qquad (6.37)$$

$$\sum_i \sum_n T_{ij}^n = D_j.$$

The expenditure constraint is then

$$E^n = \sum_i \sum_j T_{ij}^n C_{ij}^n. \qquad (6.38)$$

Trip distribution for person type n is then given by

$$T_{ij}^n = O_i^n A_i^n D_j B_j e^{-b^n c_{ij}^n}. \qquad (6.39)$$

If information or forecasts were available for the total number of trips by person type n destinating in each zone, then the destination-end constraint would be

$$\sum_i T_{ij}^n = D_j^n, \qquad (6.40)$$

and trip distribution would be given by

$$T_{ij}^n = O_i^n A_i^n D_j^n B_j^n e^{-b^n c_{ij}^n}. \qquad (6.41)$$

Appendix:
An Alternative Approach to Estimating Constrained Distribution Models

The 'market-shares' form of singly constrained distribution model allows for the simultaneous estimation of coefficients on both travel-cost and land-use characteristics. A somewhat different approach to the estimation of constrained models is implicit in much conventional transportation study modelling work. This assumes that the coefficient on the land-use term in (6.13) is unity. Model estimation is then limited to fitting a so-called 'deterrence function' which describes the effects of travel cost on trip-making.

The deterrence function is obtained by relating the two sorts of frequency distribution shown in Figures 6.1 and 6.2. Figure 6.1 shows the distribution of trip-making by generalised cost. Figure 6.2 shows the

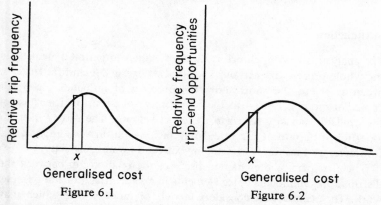

Figure 6.1

Figure 6.2

frequency distribution of trip-end opportunities, or whatever measure of land use is used in each of the generalised cost intervals, such as the xth, in Figure 6.1. By dividing the relative frequency of trips in each cost interval by the relative frequency of trip-end opportunities we obtain a series of points such as those shown in Figure 6.3. Regression or other

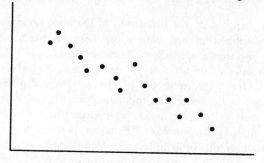

Generalised cost

Figure 6.3

estimating methods may then be used to fit a function to the points. This usually takes the form ke_{ij}^{-bc} or kc_{ij}^{-b}. In each case, the larger b is, the steeper is the slope of the deterrence function.

CHAPTER SEVEN

Modal Choice

Introduction

The analysis of modal choice is the most policy-orientated element in the whole process of analysing and forecasting the demand for travel in urban areas. In the short term, the problem of influencing people's choice of mode is central to the achievement of a more efficient use of the available capacity of urban transport systems. The achievement of an efficient pattern of use of existing facilities in turn has implications for the level of resources invested in expanding system capacity.

The first part of the chapter discusses the relationship between the distribution and modal choice elements in a sequential modelling framework. The second part considers models of mode choice which may exist in isolation from other stages of the demand analysis. A final section examines the specific problem of forecasting the impact of new travel modes.

Distribution and Mode Choice

As an aid to exposition, the discussion in the previous chapter avoided the difficult subject of the relationship between the analysis of trip distribution and modal split. Some commentators have held that there is a large measure of simultaneity in decisions about 'where to go' and 'how to get there'; the treatment of distribution and modal choice as separate stages in the sequential modelling process has therefore attracted considerable critical attention. We consider how the problem may be tackled, first, in the context of behavioural modelling, and second, in the context of the probability-maximising approach introduced in Chapter 6.

There are two preliminary points to be made. First, if the analysis is confined to the demand for vehicular travel, then trip-makers who do not have a private car available to them do not have an effective choice of mode. Much recent work on travel demand has therefore disaggregated the household population into those with car available and those without a car (or alternatively, but not quite equivalently, into car-owning and non-car-owning households). The second group are effectively captive to the public-transport mode, and the analysis of mode choice is confined to the car-available or car-owning group. If non-vehicular travel modes are included in the analysis, then of course all households will usually have a choice of mode.

Second, as was noted in the previous chapter, the unconstrained distribution model may be estimated as a combined modal-split and distribution model. The predicted total volume of $i-j$ trips by car-owning households is then the sum of predicted mode-specific trips. Alternatively, however the unconstrained model may be estimated with the volume of $i-j$ trips by all modes as the variable to be explained. The set of explanatory variables might then include the travel characteristics of both car and public-transport modes. Derivation of the modal shares in turn would require the sequential application of a modal-choice model.

In principle, the same alternatives of simultaneous or sequential treatment of distribution and modal choice are available within the 'full' sequential process embodying a singly or doubly constrained distribution model, although until quite recently the standard procedure has been to estimate distribution and modal choice sequentially. Thus in the singly constrained case, trip distribution would be carried out using a model of the following kind:

$$T_{ij} = O_i A_i D_j f(C_{ij}). \tag{7.1}$$

Modal split would then be estimated as

$$\frac{T_{ijk}}{\sum_k T_{ijk}} = \frac{g(C_{ijk})}{\sum_k g(C_{ijk})}. \tag{7.2}$$

For example, if

$$g(C_{ijk}) = e^{-\lambda C_{ijk}},$$

and there were only two alternative modes, car and public transport, then

$$\frac{T_{ij}^{CAR}}{T_{ij}^{CAR} + T_{ij}^{PT}} = \frac{1}{1 + e^{-\lambda(C_{ij}^{PT} - C_{ij}^{CAR})}} \tag{7.3}$$

λ would be estimated cross-sectionally by using the observed set of $(C_{ij}^{PT} - C_{ij}^{CAR})$ values. The form of diversion curve represented by (7.3) is shown in Figure 7.1.

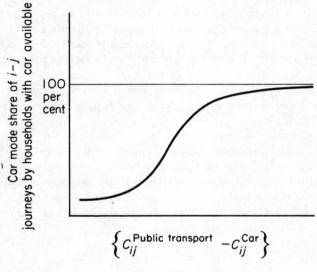

Figure 7.1

With a model of this kind, the elasticity of modal share (S_{ijk}) with respect to own or other mode cost, (C_{ijk}/S_{ijk}) $(\delta S_{ijk}/\delta C_{ijk})$ may be estimated as

$$\frac{-\lambda C_{ijk}\, e^{-\lambda(C_{ijm} - C_{ijk})}}{1 + e^{-\lambda(C_{ijm} - C_{ijk})}}.$$

Thus, the higher is λ, the more sensitive is modal split to cost differences.

The main difficulty with this approach lies in the specification of the cost or impedance term in the distribution model. Two alternative specifications have been suggested, each based on a different hypothesis about people's perception of cost when more than one mode is available. On the first view, the relevant cost is that of the least-cost mode, which in most situations is the car mode. The alternative view, found in the SELNEC Transportation Study, for example,[1] is that the cost used in the distribution model should be a function of the costs of the alternative available modes.

The SELNEC model therefore used a so-called 'composite impedence' term of the form

$$e^{-bC_{ij}} = \frac{1}{m} \sum_k e^{-bC_{ijk}}, \qquad (7.4)$$

where m = the number of available modes (in the SELNEC case, two).

If, in practice, it was not possible to travel by public transport from i to j, then the public-transport cost was given an arbitrarily large value.[2] In the two-mode case the composite impedance term can be written as

$$e^{-bC_{ij}} = \tfrac{1}{2}(e^{-bC_{ij1}} + e^{-bC_{ij2}}), \qquad (7.5)$$

and

$$C_{ij} = C_{ij1} - \frac{1}{b} \log \tfrac{1}{2}(1 + e^{-b(C_{ij1} - C_{ij2})}). \qquad (7.6)$$

It can be seen that as $C_{ij2} \to \infty$, then

$$e^{-bC_{ij}} \to \tfrac{1}{2} e^{-bC_{ij1}} \qquad (7.7)$$

and

$$C_{ij} \to C_{ij1} - \frac{1}{b} \log e \frac{1}{2}. \qquad (7.8)$$

Conversely, as $C_{ij2} \to C_{ij1}$, then

$$e^{-bC_{ij}} \to e^{-bC_{ij1}} \qquad (7.9)$$

and

$$C_{ij} \to C_{ij1}. \qquad (7.10)$$

The general *a priori* restrictions which would be imposed on a composite impedance term of the kind $e^{-bC_{ij}}$ are first that it should be a decreasing function of modal availability; second, with C_{ij1} given, that it should be a decreasing function of C_{ij2}. Both of these conditions are satisfied by the formulation in (7.5) above. What is uncertain is the rate at which composite impedance should decline as the relative performance of the 'inferior' mode declines. The hypothesis that composite impedence is a function only of the generalised cost of the 'best' mode is thus the limiting case of a wide spectrum of possible specifications. No empirical testing appears to have been done of the comparative performance of alternative specifications in replicating an observed pattern of trip-making. All that can be said is that individual transportation studies which have used one or other procedure have reported satisfactory calibrations.

An equivalent form of sequential model within the probability maximising framework has been suggested by Wilson.[3] Trips are first of all distributed on the basis of the costs of the minimum cost mode between each zone pair. The $i-j$ trip volume estimated in this way is then split between modes using a diversion curve. In this formulation, the expenditure constraint is split into two elements, X and Y, where

$$X = \sum_i \sum_j T_{ij} \times X_{ij} \qquad (7.11)$$

and

$$Y = \sum_i \sum_j \sum_k T_{ijk} (C_{ijk} - X_{ij}), \qquad (7.12)$$

where X_{ij} = travel cost on the minimum cost mode between i and j.

This form of model assumes therefore that a certain proportion of the total travel budget is spent in, as Wilson puts it, 'achieving destinations'. The remainder is spent on travel by other than the minimum cost mode.

The distribution model is therefore estimated with an expenditure constraint of the form given by (7.11) above. The expression for T_{ij} is then

$$T_{ij} = O_i A_i D_j B_j e^{-bx_{ij}}. \qquad (7.13)$$

The modal split model then solves for T_{ijk} subject to an expenditure constraint given by (7.17) above, and the constraint that

$$\sum_k T_{ijk} = T_{ij}. \qquad (7.14)$$

It follows that

$$T_{ijk} = e^{-\lambda^2} \times e^{-\lambda^1} (C_{ijk} - x_{ij}). \qquad (7.15)$$

Thus

$$\sum_k T_{ijk} = e^{1\lambda^2} \times \sum_k e^{-\lambda^1}(C_{ijk} - x_{ijk}). \qquad (7.16)$$

Hence, the diversion curve is given by

$$\frac{T_{ijk}}{\sum\limits_k T_{ijk}} = \frac{e^{-\lambda^1} C_{ijk}}{\sum\limits_k e^{-\lambda^1} C_{ijk}} . \qquad (7.17)$$

As with the 'distribution-only' version of the probability-maximising model presented in the previous chapter, the values of b and λ 'fall out' of the modelling process once the expenditure constraints have been given. The use of the probability-maximising procedure for forecasting therefore involves predicting the values of X and Y. We have already pointed out that little is known about the behaviour of aggregate 'expenditure' over time where this includes both money and time outlays; even less is known about changes in the share of expenditure allocated to 'achieving destinations' over time.

The sequential treatment of distribution and ,modal split may be written as a market-shares model taking the form (singly constrained):

$$T_{ijk} = O_i \left\{ \frac{D_j f(\sum\limits_k C_{ijk})}{\sum\limits_j D_j f(\sum\limits_k C_{ijk})} \right\} \left\{ \frac{g(C_{ijk})}{\sum\limits_k g(C_{ijk})} \right\} . \qquad (7.18)$$

Writing

$$S_{ij} = \frac{D_j f(\sum\limits_k C_{ijk})}{\sum\limits_j D_j f(\sum\limits_k C_{ijk})}$$

and

$$S_{ijk} = \frac{g(C_{ijk})}{\sum\limits_k g(C_{ijk})} \qquad (7.19)$$

the expression for T_{ijk} can be written as

$$T_{ijk} = O_i \times S_{ij} \times S_{ijk}. \qquad (7.20)$$

This form of the market-shares model perhaps emphasises the behavioural hypothesis underlying it: that decisions on 'where to go' precede decisions on 'how to get there'. A different form of market-shares model would be produced if we made the alternative hypothesis that choice of mode preceded choice of destination. The model would then take the following form:

$$T_{ijk} = O_i \times S_{ik} \times S_{kij}. \qquad (7.21)$$

In this form the term S_{ik} could imply a mode-specific trip-generation model. The term S_{kij} can be written as a mode-specific distribution model of the following kind:

$$S_{kij} = \frac{D_{jk}\, f_k\, (C_{ijk})}{\sum\limits_{j} D_{jk}\, f_k\, (C_{ijk})}. \qquad (7.22)$$

Note that the use of mode-specific trip-distribution models requires some form of mode-split model in the forecasting context.

Now suppose that we wish to compare the changes in travel behaviour resulting from a change in transport-network costs predicted by the two forms of model given by (7.20) and (7.21). We assume that both are estimated on the same set of ijk observations. The derivatives of (7.20) and (7.21) with respect to C_{ijk} are, respectively:

$$\frac{\partial T_{ijk}}{\partial C_{ijk}} = O_i \left\{ S_{ijk}\, \frac{\partial S_{ij}}{\partial C_{ijk}} + S_{ij}\, \frac{\partial S_{ijk}}{\partial C_{ijk}} \right\}$$

and

$$\frac{\partial T_{ijk}}{\partial C_{ijk}} = O_i \left\{ S_{ik}\, \frac{\partial S_{kij}}{\partial C_{ijk}} + S_{kij}\, \frac{\partial S_{ik}}{\partial C_{ijk}} \right\} \qquad (7.23)$$

Only by coincidence will these two expressions be equal. This implies that the forecasts of trip volume changes in a sequential modelling procedure will usually be strongly dependent on the sequencing of the model.[4]

However, if the parameters of the generalised cost term in the distribution and modal-split models are equal, then this is a sufficient condition for the outcome of the forecasting process to be independent of sequencing. In fact it transforms the sequential model into a simultaneous one since

$$\frac{T_{ijk}}{O_i} = \left\{ \frac{D_j f(\sum_k C_{ijk})}{\sum_j D_j f(\sum_k C_{ijk})} \right\} \left\{ \frac{g(C_{ijk})}{\sum_k g(C_{ijk})} \right\} \tag{7.24}$$

$$= \frac{D_j f(C_{ijk})}{\sum_j \sum_k D_j f(C_{ijk})} . \tag{7.25}$$

This general form of model is similar to Luce's so-called 'strict utility model'[5] in which the relative probability of any option *ijk* is given by the ratio of the attributes of *ijk* to those of the set of relevant alternatives to *ijk*. Satisfaction of this strict utility condition in turn guarantees the path independence of measures of benefit of transport-network changes (discussed in Chapter 9).

Unfortunately, given the current state of the art it is not possible to say with any confidence that the simultaneous (or rational) form of model is a better basis for predicting people's behaviour than one based on a sequential structure.

The 'strict utility' form of model does emphasise one thing which is relevant to the subsequent discussion of new modes. If we define the probability of choosing option *ijk* from the set of alternatives X as

$$P(ijk: X) = \frac{g_{ijk}}{\sum_{ijk \in X} g_{ijk}} , \tag{7.26}$$

then it should be emphasised that X is the set of *relevant* alternatives. It can be easily seen that the probability of choosing *ijk* may be sensitive to the definition of this set.

Returning to an earlier theme, the discussion in Chapter 6 and the present chapter has highlighted a fundamental difference in approach between behaviourally based models and those using a probability-maximising approach. The use of behavioural models for forecasting distribution and modal split requires no more than an assumption that the estimated parameters of the relevant functions are approximately constant through time. The probability-maximising approach, on the other hand, requires forecasts of the relevant expenditure constraints. As we have argued, this is currently a very much under-researched area. At the moment, therefore, there is no basis for predicting what total expenditure will be, or how it might alter in response to changes in the relative costs of different modes. We must therefore conclude that, despite its considerable *a priori* attractions, the probability-maximising approach to travel forecasting is an empty box at its current stage of development. Nevertheless, it has potential advantages over the behavioural approach, in particular its ability to handle a generalised cost function in a way which is independent of choice of cost units. The prescription here is not to dismiss the whole approach but rather for further research to provide a basis for forecasting the relevant inputs so that it can be made operational and its predictions compared with those of the behavioural approach.

Disaggregated Mode-Choice Models

The following three aspects of disaggregated mode choice models are discussed:

(1) the level of spatial aggregation at which they are estimated;
(2) the form of model developed; and
(3) use of the models to obtain empirical estimates of values of time.

Spatial Aggregation

The analysis of urban travel demands described so far has explained and predicted travel behaviour at an aggregative level. Much of the specific analysis of mode choice, however, has been disaggregative in nature, examining mode-choice decisions either by individuals or households.

The main argument against the use of models calibrated using zonal average data relates essentially to the problem of within-zone and between-zone variability in the variables which may affect choice of mode. This argument echoes that presented in Chapter 4 on trip generation and attraction. Thus, especially if zone sizes are relatively large, the within-zone variability of public-transport access times may well be higher than variability between zones. The importance of such variables in determining choice of mode may well be understated in analysis using zonal data, and for this reason it seems desirable to use disaggregative models in attempting to estimate the implicit values placed by travellers on the elements of over-all journey time described in Chapter 5.

Form of Model

The expression for the generalised cost of travel developed in Chapter 5 was of the following form:

$$c_k = m_k + \sum_x v^x t_k^x. \tag{7.27}$$

Disaggregated modal-choice models usually examine individual decisions about which mode to choose on the assumption that a prior decision has been taken to make a trip to a particular destination. Given this assumption, it may be assumed that the trip-end utility derived by the individual is independent of choice of mode. The individual's choice of mode may therefore be characterised as a cost-minimisation problem in which the cost has a number of dimensions corresponding to the potential sources of 'disutility'. The more obvious of these are the expenditure of money and time which are allowed for on the generalised cost formulation in (7.27) above. However, there may be others, in particular discomfort or unreliability which are not specified.[6]

If we reformulate (7.27) above in terms of the nth individual, then he will choose mode k in preference to mode 1 if

$$c_k^n < c_1^n,$$

that is if

$$m_k^n + \sum_x v_x^n t_{xk} < m_1^n + \sum_x v_x^n t_{x1}.$$

The problem is that v_x^n cannot be observed but only inferred from individual mode choices. However, v_x^n is likely to vary between individuals, and it is also possible that individuals may misperceive both m_k and m_1 and t_k^x and t_1^x. This immediately poses a further problem for modal-choice work. Should the estimation process be based upon 'engineering' or 'perceived' values of m and t? A major constraint in practice has often been the non-availability of data on alternative perceived mode performance from surveys. *Faute de mieux*, therefore, engineering data has often been used.

The objective of modal-choice models is to estimate the parameter values which best explain individuals' observed mode choices given observed (engineering) values of the explanatory variable. The form of estimating model used in the analysis thus stems from the probabilistic nature of the model being estimated and the fact that the individual usually chooses between two alternative modes.

It is assumed that if the estimated disutility function for the population as a whole is a linear function, $G(x)$, of the components of disutility, then the probability of an individual choosing mode 1 will be

$$P_1 = \frac{e^{G(x)}}{1 + e^{G(x)}} .$$ (7.28)

This describes a so-called 'sigmoid response' curve of the form shown in Figure 7.2. $G(x)$ is estimated using observed modal choices and observed values for the explanatory variables. The form of (7.28) above for the car – public-transport mode choice will be

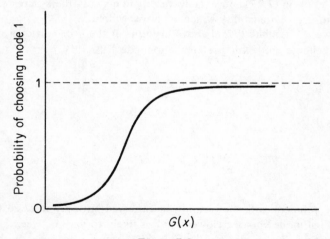

Figure 7.2

$$P_{CAR} = \frac{\exp \left(b_0 + b_1 \left(x_1^{CAR} - x_1^{PT}\right) \ldots + b_n \left(x_n^{CAR} - x_n^{PT}\right)\right)}{1 + \exp \left(b_0 + \left(x_1^{CAR} - x_1^{PT}\right) \ldots + b_n \left(x_n^{CAR} - x_n^{PT}\right)\right)}$$ (7.29)

$$= \frac{e^{X_{CAR}}}{e^{X_{CAR}} + e^{X_{PT}}}$$ (7.30)

multiplying both numerator and the nominator of equation (7.29) by $e^{X_{PT}}$, where $X_{CAR} = b_0 + b_1 \times x_1^{CAR} \ldots + b_n \times x_n^{CAR}$ and

$$X_{PT} = b_1 \times x_1^{PT} \ldots b_n \times x_n^{PT}.$$

Thus if the constant term is non-zero, then the probability of the car mode being chosen when $\Delta xb = 0$ is greater than or less than according to the sign of the constant term.

The statistical techniques which may be used to fit sigmoid curves have been extensively discussed elsewhere.[7] It will be noticed that the functional form given by the sigmoid curve is similar to the form of modal-split function used in aggregative work described by equation (7.3) above.

If a generalised cost expression is at the aggregate level, then the calibration of the modal-choice function involves the estimation of a single modal-split parameter, λ in equation (7.3). It follows that if in the aggregative relationship $C_{CAR} = C_{PT}$, then $P_{CAR} = \frac{1}{2}$. In practice, in calibrating a modal-split model of this form, a constant is added to the generalised cost, usually of the public-transport mode, to take account of the 'unobserved' advantages of the car mode which are not reflected in the generalised cost expression.

If generalised cost is not used, then the calibration of the modal-split function using aggregative data involves an estimation process exactly analogous to the fitting of functions to individual data. At the aggregate level the $G(x)$ function may be estimated using regression methods, with the variable to be explained in the form

$$\log \left\{ \frac{P_k^{ij}}{1 - P_k^{ij}} \right\} ,$$

where P_k^{ij} = proportion of ij travellers using the kth mode.

A major practical problem in many small and medium-sized towns is that the estimation of the modal-split function (whether using individual or zonal average data) is based on a set of extreme observed values. This is often the case where the following conditions apply:

(1) car parking is free or available at low cost and there are no physical constraints on availability; and

(2) journey lengths are relatively short.

Together these guarantee that the car mode is usually both cheaper (in terms of perceived operating costs) and quicker than the public-transport mode. Under these conditions, car availability is virtually synonymous with car use. The existence of an effective choice or trade-off situation between modes in which one mode is quicker but more expensive than the other for at least some ij pairs is required for a meaningful calibration of a modal-split model. Unless this is the case, then in terms of the sigmoid curve, we are observing choices (or proportions) at the extreme right-hand end of the distribution in Figure 7.2.

Evidence on Parameter Values

The function $G(X)$ in the modal-split model

$$\frac{e^{G(X)}}{1 + e^{G(X)}}$$

may be written as a linear function of differences between modes in the observable aspects of their performance such as cost m, in-vehicle time i, access time a, and wait time w:

$$G(X) = b_0 + b_1 \Delta m + b_2 \Delta i + b_3 \Delta a + b_4 \Delta w. \qquad (7.31)$$

It is argued that if a unit change in Δm produces a change in $G(X)$ of b_1 and a unit change in Δi produces a change in $G(X)$ of b_2, then the increment in i is implicitly valued at b_1/b_2 times whatever money unit is being used. By a similar argument, it follows that the ratios b_1/b_2 and b_1/b_4 represent the 'weightings' placed on access and wait times.

The more important empirical results of studies in this field have been discussed in Chapter 5.

At this point we may note that there is a real difficulty in interpreting the value of b_1/b_2 times the money unit as a value of time spent travelling in any particular mode. De Donnea, for example, points out that if one mode has different comfort characteristics from another, then the choice of that mode reflects not only a 'pure' value of time but a valuation of the circumstances under which the travel time is spent.[8] On the other hand it is suggested that the constant term in $G(X)$ is taking account of unobserved differences, such as comfort, between modes.

The Analysis of New Modes

The disaggregated models of mode choice discussed above are binary in form implying that for a trip to any given destination, the individual is confronted by only two modes of travel. Conventionally these two modes have been a public-transport mode and car. In practice, however, the user may have more than two modes to choose from. For example, there may be more than one public-transport mode available, or alternatively he may choose to walk or cycle as an alternative to using either vehicle mode.

The existence of more than two competing modes introduces a problem of the appropriate structure with which to analyse travel decisions. The 'decision-tree' concept has been developed as a means of analysing problems of this kind. If, for example, two public-transport modes and a private-car mode are available for the journey, then we can identify two alternative forms of decision tree shown in Figure 7.3.

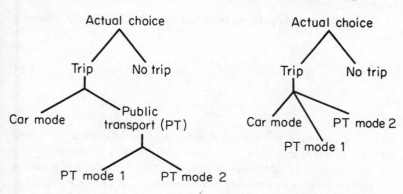

Figure 7.3 Alternative forms of decision tree

In the first, the consumer is envisaged as making an initial choice between public and private transport; if public transport is chosen, a further choice is made on the form of public transport. In the second, the consumer is viewed as choosing simultaneously between the three available modes. In other words, the first form of decision tree breaks the decision-making process down into a series of binary choices, the second form treats the decision-making as a choice between multiple alternatives.

These alternative forms of decision-making processes produce differently specified modal-choice models in situations where more than two public-transport modes are available. Taking the exponentially weighted form of model, for example, the binary choice model would produce a modal-split model of the following kind:

$$\frac{T^{\text{CAR}}}{\Sigma T} = \frac{e^{\lambda_1 x\text{CAR}}}{e^{\lambda_1 x\text{CAR}} + e^{\lambda_1 x\text{PT}}} \qquad (7.32)$$

$$\frac{T^{\text{BUS}}}{T^{\text{PT}}} = \frac{e^{\lambda_2 x\text{BUS}}}{e^{\lambda_2 x\text{BUS}} + e^{\lambda_2 x\text{RAIL}}}. \qquad (7.33)$$

The form of $e^{\lambda x\text{PT}}$ in (7.32) remains undetermined. The problem is similar to the choice of c in the distribution model; the obvious forms are the characteristics of the 'best' PT mode, or the weighted characteristics of the alternatives.

The simultaneous model on the other hand would take the following form:

$$\frac{T^{\text{CAR}}}{\sum_k T} = \frac{e^{\lambda_1 x\text{CAR}}}{\sum_k e^{\lambda_1 x_k}}. \qquad (7.34)$$

The choice between these alternative forms of model in situations where multiple rather than binary choices are available may be determined by the 'goodness of fit' of alternative model forms. The problem posed by the introduction of a new mode in a situation where choice has hitherto been binary in nature is that there is no *a priori* means of specifying which of the alternative modal-split procedures is the more efficient. Certainly the predicted share of the new mode is sensitive to the choice of model. If the new mode is a new public-transport mode, then the sequential binary form of model will lead to lower predicted patronage than the simultaneous model. In particular, the sequential form of model is likely to minimise the extent of diversion from car mode. For example, if the first stage of the sequential form of model uses the 'best' public transport mode characteristics, and the new mode is 'inferior' to the existing public-transport mode, then the car share of total trip-making remains unchanged and the new mode takes patronage exclusively from the existing public-transport mode. Some comparative results of applying these alternative forms of model have been presented by McFadden.[9]

The alternative modes available in most urban situations allow for a fairly clear distinction to be made between public and private transport. This suggests that the binary choice model may be the more realistic one in urban conditions.

CHAPTER EIGHT

Assignment

The distribution and modal-split elements of the sequential process are based upon a set of 'trial' values of the travel costs for each $i-j-k$ relationship. The objective of the assignment process is to achieve consistency between the pattern of demand produced by these trial values and the supply characteristics of the transport network. Assignment therefore involves the conversion of a set of mode-specific person journeys between zone pairs into a set of vehicular journeys on links in the modelled transport network. The volume assigned to each link must then be made consistent with the supply characteristics of the link.

Thus if the processes of generation, distribution and modal split produce a matrix of travel demands T_{ijk}^0 with an exogenously given matrix of travel costs, C_{ijk}^0, the assignment process results in a matrix of travel costs, C_{ijk}^1 which is consistent with the demand T_{ijk}^0, given the supply characteristics. This is shown in figure 8.1.

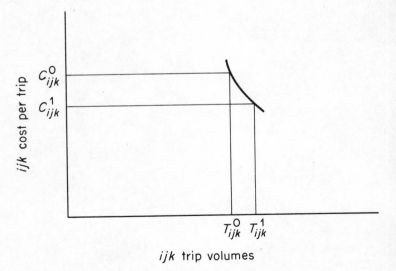

Figure 8.1

As was pointed out in Chapter 3, the process could then be iterated back to the demand system and a new set of demands, T_{ijk}^1, consistent with the cost matrix, C_{ijk}^1 produced. We noted that, in practice, this process of iteration between demand and assignment in a sequential analysis process is costly. Whatever the number of iterations undertaken, the matrix of costs, C_{ijk}^n, together with the set of demands, T_{ijk}^{n-1}, provide the inputs to the evaluation process.

More detailed discussion of the assignment process now follows, covering the following topics-

(1) categories of person journey not assigned to the network;
(2) the specification of the supply characteristics;
(3) assignment and routing, and
(4) public-transport assignment.

An appendix discusses work on junction delays and its possible relevance to transport modelling in more detail.

Person Journeys Not Assigned to the Network

There are two points to make here. First, only vehicular journeys are assigned to the networks, the assumption being that the costs of non-vehicular journeys are unaffected by their volume or by the volume of vehicular mode journeys. This has potentially quite important implications if non-vehicular as well as vehicular modes are represented in the modelling. However, it has not usually been the practice for 'strategic' urban transportation studies to separately model walk and cycle trips. Second, only inter-zonal journeys are assigned to the network. Intra-zonal trips (represented by the principle diagonal in the trip-making matrix) are given a notional cost for use in the distribution stage of the modelling process, and it is assumed that this cost also remains invariant with respect to changes in the volume of flows on the modelled network.

Supply-Side Specification

The conventional approach to the specification of the supply side is based on link speed - flow functions, of the kind shown in Figure 8.2. A family of such functions may be defined, relating average vehicle speed to the level of flow on a link, with characteristics related to those of the link itself. Thus in Figure 8.2, the function $K_0 - A_0 - B_0$ might apply to a dual-carriageway road in suburban conditions; $K_1 - A_1 - B_1$

might represent a two-lane, two-way road in a central urban area. K_0 and K_1 are the free flow speeds, F_0 and F_1 the flows at which additional vehicles start to reduce the average speeds achieved by other vehicles, and F_0(max) and F_1(max) the maximum link capacities. If user costs are expressed as a function of speed (or travel time), then a set of journey (or link) cost functions may be defined relating average cost per journey to the number of journeys made on a link.

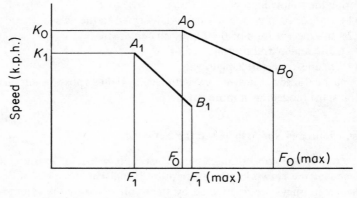

Figure 8.2

The conventional speed – flow approach breaks down in cases where the number of journeys assigned to a link per unit of time exceeds the link capacity given by the F(max) point. If the supply side is specified in terms of costs as a function of flows along links, then once the maximum capacity of a link has been reached the cost function becomes vertical, as in Figure 8.3. In these circumstances, if demand is not to exceed supply, some kind of 'shadow price' has to be imposed, shown by $(P_1 - P_0)$ in Figure 8.3. In the original London Transportation Study, for example, a linear programming procedure was developed in order to remove 'excess' trips, which were then either suppressed or re-assigned to public-transport modes.[1] Some work on the economics of roads even reported backward-bending supply functions when supply was expressed in terms of flow per unit of time.[2]

More recently, a clearer understanding of the appropriate specification for the cost function has been achieved by noting that excess demand at certain points in the road network may be accommodated in

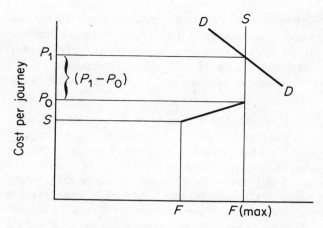

Figure 8.3

the form of queues.[3] Once this is recognised then it is apparent that the journey - cost function can be extended beyond the point of maximum output per time period, as in Figure 8.4, with the curve beyond $F(\text{max})$ representing the effect of queuing delays — principally on users' journey times. The cost function is then expressed in terms of cost per journey demanded in a specified time period.

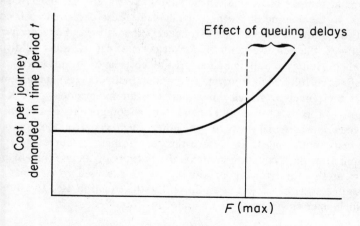

Journeys demanded in time period *t*

Figure 8.4

Conventional speed – flow functions have therefore been adapted to take account of queuing delays. Thus the F(max) point may be more or less explicitly related to the junction capacities of the link being represented; while beyond the F(max) point a tail has been added to take account of queuing delays. However, as a current D.O.E. *Advice Note* points out:[4]

> The speeds indicated in the curves are assumed to be based on travel times from junction centre to junction centre, taking nominal account only of junction delays except in the case of the curves for suburban roads where junction delays have been allowed for. It is recognised that this virtual disregard of junction delays is inaccurate and makes no allowance for their very considerable congestion effect (which may well be of greater importance in urban areas than the inter junction flows) but this is accepted until further advice on junction delays in the transportation study context is available.

If, as this appears to be suggesting, travel times through a network are largely determined by junction frequencies and capacities, then it would seem desirable that network descriptions should take more explicit account of junction characteristics. In the longer term, it is perhaps worth considering whether network description should not be based on junctions, with 'links' merely serving as junction connectors.[5]

The journey cost function appropriate to the analysis of supply – demand interaction is one which relates the travel costs perceived by users to the volume of journeys demanded. These perceived costs consist of both time and out-of-pocket expenditures. For car mode journeys, the perceived out-of-pocket costs of car use must be distinguished from the full marginal private costs and the resource costs (defined as full marginal private costs minus indirect taxes). It is assumed that the perceived vehicle operating costs are independent of link (or journey) speeds. On the other hand, several components of the full or engineering marginal costs of vehicle use, such as petrol consumption, do vary with speed. Because estimates of these resource costs are required in the evaluation context, the outputs of the assignment process in the form of link or journey speeds are used to estimate the resource costs of car journeys. Currently, the equation used to estimate vehicle operating costs takes the following form:[6]

$$c = a + \frac{b}{v} + cv^2, \qquad (8.1)$$

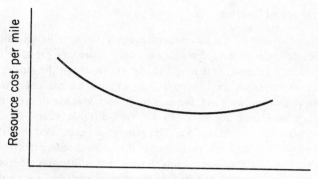

Figure 8.5

where v = vehicle speed, and c = resource cost per vehicle mile. As currently estimated in best-practice U.K. work, this takes the form shown in Figure 8.5. The minimum cost is reached at an average speed of approximately 40 m.p.h. For a link of m units, (8.1) can be re-expressed as

$$c = am + b't + c'\frac{m^3}{t^2},$$ (8.2)

where t = journey time. The relationship between b and b' and c and c' depends upon the units in which travel time and speed are measured.

Finally, it is perhaps worth noting that the resource cost expression given by equations (8.1) and (8.2) is relevant for defining the marginal social cost function used in discussions of optimal pricing. Total link cost per journey is obtained by adding time costs to the equation (8.2) for vehicle operating cost. Total social cost is then the summation of this over all journeys demanded:

$$T = q\left(vt + am + bt + c\,\frac{m^3}{t^2} \right),$$ (8.3)

where T = total social cost, v = value of time, t = link journey time = $t(q)$, and q = journeys demanded. Marginal social cost is then equal to the derivative of (8.3) with respect to q. In uncongested (free-flow) conditions, the derivative of t with respect to q is 0, so that marginal social cost equals average social cost. In these conditions it is possible that perceived costs may exceed social costs, but in congested conditions the opposite will usually be true.

Assignment and Routing

The main features of the assignment process can best be explained by reference to a diagram representing a road network of the kind used in the modelling process. This may help to explain both the nature of the network descriptions used in modelling and the assignment process itself. Suppose that we have forecast a certain volume of trips moving between zone i, with access to the network at node A, and zone j with access to the network at node E. The generalised cost used to distribute the journeys will be some estimate of the generalised cost involved in traversing the links between i and j plus any additional 'access costs' involved in getting from the hypothetical zone centroid on to the network at the origin end and off it to the zone centroid at the destination end. The generalised cost will be based upon the link lengths and the expected travel times required to traverse each of the links. In the case shown in Figure 8.6, the problem of deciding exactly which route to take is an easy one; there is only one feasible route. Therefore, all the journeys between A and E will be assigned to links AB, BC, CD, and DE.

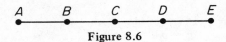

Figure 8.6

However, in the more complex networks typical of urban areas, such a simple solution will not usually be found. A more complex type of network linking A and E is shown in Figure 8.7. Here it is apparent that there are a number of alternative routes between A and E which might be chosen. For example, the routing might be *ABCDE*, ABCFE, *ABGFE*, or even *ABCGFE*. In general, the costs associated with each of these routes will be different, although perhaps not very significantly so.

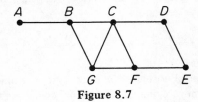

Figure 8.7

Early studies used what is known as 'all-or-nothing' (or unconstrained) assignments based on the route with the minimum free-flow journey time between zones. If, in Figure 8.7, *ABCDE* had a lower journey time than the other routes, then all journeys between A and E

would be assigned to it; similarly, all journeys from *B* to *E* would be assigned to the route *BCDE*. More recently, the somewhat restrictive assumption that minimum cost or travel time routes are chosen (reflecting something like perfect knowledge on the part of drivers) has been relaxed by the development of so-called 'multiple routing' techniques.[7] The general principle of multiple routing can be seen by reference to Figure 8.8. There are three alternative routes from both *A* and *B* to *E*. Each link, *AC, CG* etc. is characterised by an actual link cost, and on this basis it would normally be possible to define a minimum cost route. Given the actual costs in the diagram, this minimum cost route would be *ACDE*, costing 52 units. The alternatives, *ACGFE*, and *ACGDE* cost 54 and 60 units respectively.

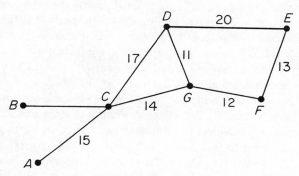

Figure 8.8

The multiple routing procedure assumes, in effect, a distribution of costs around the actual or average for each link; for simplicity's sake it is assumed that the range is from plus to minus 2. Having defined a number of feasible routes, the link times on each route are, so to speak, randomised; the simplest way of thinking of this process is to say that the link cost used in route selection, c, is equal to

$$\overline{c} + 2k,$$

where k is a random number with $\left\{ -1 \leqslant k \leqslant 1 \right\}$. Assume for simplicity that the randomised set of link times are 15, 18.5 and 21 for *ACDE*; and 15, 13.5 and 12.5 for *ACGFE*. The total cost for *ACDE* will exceed that of *ACGFE*, and journeys between nodes *A* and *E* will be assigned to the latter route.

There are three main reasons why the multiple routing procedure seems to be an improvement over previous all-or-nothing methods.

(i) From an operational point of view, it produces a more rapid convergence process than minimum-cost techniques, especially in cases where a substantial number of links in the network are operating close to capacity. For example, where there are approximately parallel routes available between areas comprising a number of origin/destination zones, the convergence processes employed in assignment might produce arbitrarily switching of routes between assignments for large blocks of traffic form a set of adjacent origin zones. With multiple routing procedures, on the other hand, there is likely to be a more even spread of trips on the alternative routes, so that the amount of switching taking place between iterations is substantially reduced.

(ii)   The use of multiple routing also appears to satisfy plausible *a priori* behavioural hypotheses more satisfactorily than the simple minimum-cost routing procedure in a number of respects. The first is that the individual user's perception of the 'costs' involved on alternative routes is likely to be subject to imperfect information, certainly in a densely developed and congested urban network. It may be hypothesised, for example, that the perceived cost on which a route choice decision is taken is a function of an average cost and the variance of cost or journey time. If the achieved journey cost on one alternative route appears to be subject to substantial variation, then search activities may be instituted to find routes with perhaps higher average achieved cost but lower variation. This might produce quite variable patterns of route choice for the individual, and hence for a spread of routings for a population of individuals. The second point is that the cost item used to define link costs is in fact an average for the population of users; the elements of generalised cost relevant to route choice are the time and distance/out-of-pocket costs. In the same way as in modal-choice situations, users may be confronted by a choice between a longer but faster route and a shorter but slower route. Suppose that on the basis of average perceived values of time and movement cost, the first alternative has a somewhat lower cost than the second. Nevertheless, we would expect to find some people with a relatively low value of time choosing the second (slower) route. It might be added that the scope for potential trade-offs of this kind is perhaps more obvious in inter-urban than in an urban context.[5]

(iii) There is another form of aggregation problem, this time an areal one. The modelling process deals in terms of movements from 'areal aggregates' — zones, each containing a number of individual origin and destination points. Whilst it is assumed that trips arise and destinate at a single node point for each zone, it will usually be the case that there are a number of alternative 'real' access points to the network represented in the assignment model. The use of different access points may give rise to a different pattern of route choice, which can only be satisfactorily represented in a 'randomised' fashion.

Multiple-Mode Assignment and the Definition of Public-Transport Networks

Early assignment exercises were restricted to the modelling of car journeys only. More recently, procedures have been developed for modelling public-transport networks and hence of assigning public-transport journeys.[8] The generalised cost of a public-transport journey between zones i and j can be specified in the following way:

$$C_{ij} = k + md_{ij} + v^1 t_{ij}^1 + v^2 t_{ij}^2 + v^3 t_{ij}^3, \qquad (8.4)$$

where k = constant, or boarding penalty, $d_{ij} = i - j$ distance, m = fare per unit of distance, $t_{ij}^1 = i - j$ in-vehicle travel time, t_{ij}^2 = waiting time, t_{ij}^3 = access times at boarding point, and v^i = valuation of ith journey time element.

A public-transport network description will therefore embody each of these elements. The way in which this is done is to define a network as a set of links and nodes, with zonal access times associated with each node or boarding point, and a set of headway times or service frequencies for each route. The capacity of the system is defined in terms of the service frequency times the carrying capacity of the vehicles. This latter point generates certain obvious difficulties, since the service frequency characteristics of a single node point may depend on the intended destination, if the node is used by more than one route. This is illustrated in Figure 8.9. Route 1 goes from A through E and D to B. Route 2 goes from F through E and D to C. Assume that each route

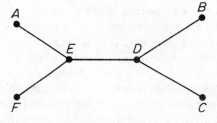

Figure 8.9

has the same average service frequency. The average vehicle headways at *E* and *D* will be half those of the other nodes in the system, but this higher service frequency will only be relevant to *E - D* or *D* journeys. The potential complexity of network description can be seen if another route is added which begins at *D* and goes through *B*. In theory, then, a passenger at *E* headed for *B* can board a route-2 vehicle and then change at *D* as an alternative to a through journey on route 1.

Taking each of the cost items in turn, and relating them to the network description activity:

(i) The fare structure for public transport is usually in the form of a step function of the kind shown in Figure 8.10. The form specified in

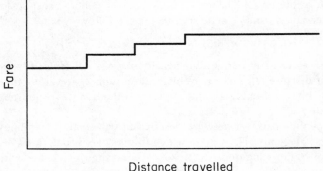

Distance travelled

Figure 8.10

(8.4) above is therefore an approximation. It ignores the stepped nature except for the initial step or boarding penalty. Moreover, the smoothed step function would be curvilinear, that is the marginal cost per unit distance falls with journey length. However, for most cases it is found that the form of cost expression in (8.4) is accurate enough.

(ii) The estimated value of the t^1 component is based on a conventional assumption about average headway speeds, which to date have been assumed to be approximately invariant with respect to network loadings for modelling purposes. That is to say, whilst public-transport vehicles are loaded on to highway networks in the assignment stage of the modelling process, there is often no feedback from highway speed–flow relationships to public-transport headway speeds. With reserved access or fixed-track public-transport systems, of course, this is a valid assumption, but clearly it is not the case for bus systems which compete with private. vehicles for road space. It might be argued that this biases the process in favour of public-transport journeys, which clearly it does to some extent. However, the importance of this point in practice may be limited for the same reason that the exact specification of public-transport fare structure is held to be relatively unimportant — the fact that the in-vehicle time component is only a part of the total generalised cost expression.

(iii) The t^2 component is usually expressed as one-half vehicle head-way time, on the assumption of a random arrival pattern. The results of empirical work on choice of mode have supported a value of the v^2 coefficient which is substantially higher than the v^1 coefficient applied to in-vehicle time; the convention adopted in recent studies in the United Kingdom has been to set $v^2 = 2v^1$, at least for travel in leisure time. The assumption that waiting time is equal to half of vehicle head-ways may in practice be modified for low levels of service frequency where, it may be argued, the arrival pattern of users may be more similar to that for travellers on fixed-track scheduled systems. However, the precise specification of the waiting-time component in some future network options tested in transportation studies, where the general level of service is substantially lower than at present, does present substantial problems, given the relatively high cost weighting attached to this item. Another difficulty is that the actual waiting time may also depend not simply on service frequency, but on vehicle loadings. If the sum of arrivals at node points in any period of time is greater than the carrying capacity of the vehicles on the route, then the result would be the formation of excess queues at stops, in the same way that excess vehicle queues form at junctions where the flow of entrance exceeds junction capacity. Effective waiting time in these circumstances may be double or even treble the 'half-headway' value.

The general effect of these various conventions on relative weightings can be illustrated for the case of a hypothetical public-transport jour-ney to work with the following characteristics:

(i)   distance travelled in-vehicle — 2 miles;
(ii) average vehicle speed — 10 m.p.h.;
(iii) walking time - 3 minutes at each end of journey;
(iv) vehicle headway — 10 minutes.

The assumptions about the coefficient values are as follows:

$$k = 2p, \qquad v^1 = 20p \text{ per hour};$$
$$m = 1p; \qquad v^2 = v^3 = 2v^1.$$

The generalised cost of the journey in money units is then

$$C_{ij} = 2 + 2 + \frac{(12)\,(20)}{60} + \frac{(12)\,(20)}{60} + \frac{10\,(20)}{60}$$

$$= 15\tfrac{1}{3} \text{ units.}$$

The effect of various alternative 'policy' measures on the generalised cost can be examined in the following terms:

(1) Free fares $\qquad C^2_{ij} = 11\tfrac{1}{3} \qquad \dfrac{C^2}{C^1} = 0.74;$

(2) Double M $\qquad C^2_{ij} = 17\tfrac{1}{3} \qquad \dfrac{C^2}{C^1} = 1.13;$

(3) Double journey speed $C^2_{ij} = 13\tfrac{1}{3} \qquad \dfrac{C^2}{C^1} = 0.87;$

(4) Halve service $\qquad C^2_{ij} = 18\tfrac{2}{3} \qquad \dfrac{C^2}{C^1} = 1.22;$
 frequency

(5) Double service $\qquad C^2_{ij} = 13\tfrac{2}{3} \qquad \dfrac{C^2}{C^1} = 0.89.$
 frequency

It is worth noting that in what is roughly the current situation for a peak-hour journey, the free-fares policy has the largest impact on total generalised cost. However, even a 100 per cent fare reduction produces only a 26 per cent reduction in total generalised cost.

As noted earlier, there is a degree of asymmetry between the treatment of public- and private-transport service levels in the assignment procedure; whilst public-transport vehicle movements are loaded on to road links, along with commercial vehicle movements which are not separately modelled in the same way as person journeys, and so contribute to the link speed–flow relationships for private vehicles, there is usually no iterative procedure to adjust public-transport speeds in response to varying loadings. As indicated earlier, it is not thought that this imparts serious bias into this part of the modelling process; however, some empirical verification of this point would be welcome.

Conclusion

The process of appraising urban transport projects and policies involves the specification of both demand- and supply-side relationships, brought together in the assignment process. Until now research effort has concentrated on the problems of demand-side modelling. Relatively little effort has been focused on the equally important problem involved in specifying the supply side. This relative neglect is curious in view of the fact that the estimation of the benefits from increasing system capacity are crucially dependent not simply on the position of the demand functions, but also of the cost functions.

As we have described the assignment process, the most obvious points of weakness with current procedures are in two areas. First, there is the specification of the public-transport system and its interaction with private transport. Second, there is the modelling of highway system characteristics under conditions of high levels of demand relative to capacity. In this second case, further progress will almost certainly involve greater emphasis on junction frequency and capacity as major determinants of travel times in urban conditions.

Appendix: Junction Delays[9]

In this appendix we first extend the discussion of junction delays and show how the analysis may be used in a simple case to define a marginal social cost. Second, we use the analysis of junction delays to illustrate a conceptual difficulty in assignment. This arises from the need to describe average network conditions within a discrete time interval such as the morning or evening peak hours.

Earlier discussion has defined the capacity of a link as the smaller of the exit- or entrance-node capacities. We now discuss the case where the capacity of the entrance node exceeds that of the exit node. Under these conditions, flows close to or at the maximum capacity of the entrance node will lead to queuing delays at the exit node.

Generally, if in the discrete time interval, $t, t+h$, the arrival rate $V(u)$ exceeds the junction discharge capacity, C, then the queue length at $t+h$ will be

$$Q(t+h) = \int_t^{t+h} V(u)\,du - Ch, \qquad (8.5)$$

if, for $u \leqslant t, V(u) < C$.

The delay experienced by arrivals at time n $(t < n \subset t+h)$ will be

$$D(n) = \frac{V(n)}{C} \left(\int_t^h V(u)\, du - Cn \right). \qquad (8.6)$$

In the time interval, $t, t+h$, the total delay experienced will be

$$D(t, t+h) = \int_t^{t+h} \frac{V(n)}{C} \left(\int_t^n V(u)\, du - Cn \right) dn. \qquad (8.7)$$

We now develop an expression for total delay in the case of a linear queue build-up and discharge fashion of the kind shown in Figure 8.11. The discharge capacity of the junction per unit of time is C. The arrival rate during the queue build-up period, from O to H, is $C(1 + a)$. In the post-peak period from H to h, the arrival rate is xC, with $x < 1$. The

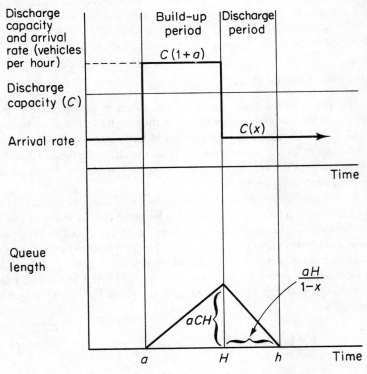

Figure 8.11

total delay over the entire period for which the junction is queued, O to h, is the sum of delays encountered during the build-up and discharge periods.

Average queue length in both build-up and discharge periods is equal to $aCH/2$, and average delay throughout the period from O to h is $ah/2$. Total delay to build-up period arrivals, D_1, is equal to

$$D_1 = H \left(\frac{aH}{2} \left(C(1 + a) \right) \right) = \frac{aCH^2}{2} (1 + a). \qquad (8.8)$$

The length of the discharge period is equal to

$$\frac{aCH}{C(1 - x)} = \frac{aH}{(1 - x)}, \qquad (8.9)$$

and hence the delay to discharge period arrivals, D_2, is equal to

$$D_2 = \left(\frac{aH}{1 - x} \right) (Cx) \left(\frac{aH}{2} \right)$$

$$= \frac{aCH^2}{2} \frac{(ax)}{1 - x}. \qquad (8.10)$$

Hence

$$D_1 + D_2 = \frac{aCH^2}{2} \left(1 + \frac{a}{1 - x} \right). \qquad (8.11)$$

The marginal delay imposed by an extra arrival during the so-called 'surcharge period' from O to H can be calculated by differentiating expression (8.11) with respect to aCH, with C and H assumed constant. This yields an expression for marginal delay equal to

$$\frac{H}{2} \left(1 + \frac{2a}{1 - x} \right). \qquad (8.12)$$

It should be noted that as $a \to 0$, $H \to 0$ so (8.12) $\to 0$. The function is therefore discontinuous at $a = 0$.

This work clearly has some conceptual interest and has pointed to the importance of junction delays in urban conditions. However, a junction-delay formula has also been used in practical appraisals of certain urban transport projects. By making assumptions about the frequency of congested junctions and about the average values of a, H and x, order of magnitude estimates may be obtained of the effects of removing some proportion of private vehicle trips.

The junction-delay model may be used to illustrate a further problem involved in assignment.

Consider a junction with a capacity of 800 vehicles per hour. The arrival rates for four 15-minute periods within a peak hour are, respectively 180, 250, 250, 150. Given this arrival pattern, a queue will start to form at the beginning of the second quarter, and will continue building until the end of the third quarter. In terms of the formula for average delays given earlier, $aH/2$, a is equal to 0.25 for the second and third quarter hours and H is equal to $\frac{1}{2}$ (in hours). However, the average for traffic arriving in the second quarter hour is equal to $aH/4$ and for third and fourth quarter arrivals it is $3aH/4$.

Thus the pattern of excess delays for the four quarter hours is as follows:

		Excess delay
1	=	0
2	=	0.03125 hours
3	=	0.09375 hours
4	=	0.09375 hours

The weighted average excess delay for the whole house is then approximately 0.05 hours. However, if the total hourly flow, 830, was used to calculate average excess delay, then a would be equal to only 0.0375 and the average delay is only approximately 0.019. The effect of taking 'average' hourly conditions is therefore to considerably underestimate the actual average delay given the intra-hour arrival pattern.

The approach most commonly used in conventional practice, as an alternative to a highly complex process of sequential modelling of successive discrete time periods, is to apply a peaking factor to the total flows taking place within, say, a two-hour peak period. This factor is often of the order of 1.1 or 1.2 depending on the definition of the peak. Applying a factor of 1.1 to the total hourly demand observed in the numerical example would produce a value for a of about 0.14 and hence an estimated average delay of 0.07 hours. A value of 1.2 on the other hand gives a value for a of 0.24 and an average delay over twice that 'observed'.

Clearly the results of assignment are likely to be highly sensitive to the assumptions made about the peaking factor; because of this we might expect that benefit estimates will be potentially sensitive to a choice of factors. Unfortunately no empirical information is available to confirm or refute this impression.

PART TWO

Evaluation

CHAPTER NINE

Economic Evaluation: The Benefit Algorithm

Introduction

The previous chapters have examined the forecasting of future travel volumes and costs in urban areas. This chapter, and the two which follow, consider the development and application of economic evaluation procedures to transport projects and policies.

The discussion in this chapter covers the following topics:

(1) the use of surplus-change measures as indicators of benefit or welfare change;

(2) the generalisation of surplus-change measures to the case where more than one price is altered simultaneously;

(3) the application of surplus-change measures in the transport sector, taking account in particular of the problems caused by cost misperception and taxation; and

(4) the benefit expression in the fixed trip matrix case.

The Use of Surplus-Change Measures

The Marshallian consumers' surplus measure of benefit is one which is extensively used in the cost-benefit analysis of transport-sector projects.[1] We first define the measure and then, by comparing it with other possible measures of benefit, identify the conditions under which it may be validly used.

The Marshallian consumers' surplus measure of the benefit of a reduction in the generalised cost of $i-j$ travel for an individual user from g_{ij}^0 to g_{ig}^1 is shown in Figure 9.1 by the shaded area. If the consumer's demand for $i-j$ travel is written as a function of the $i-j$ cost, of other costs, g, and of income, M, then, holding g and M constant, the shaded area, B, is equal to

$$-\int_{g_{ij}^0}^{g_{ij}^1} f(g_{ij}, g, M) \, dg_{ij}. \qquad (9.1)$$

We can compare this benefit measure with two alternative concepts

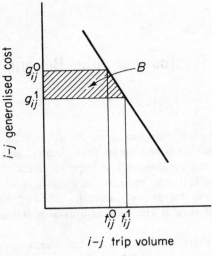

Figure 9.1

derived from the Hicksian indifference-curve analysis.[2] The first of these is the so-called 'compensating variation'. If we define an indirect utility function for our consumer of the kind

$$U = u(g_{ij}, g, M),$$ (9.2)

then the compensating variation can be defined as the change in M which would be required, following a change in g_{ij}, to leave the consumer indifferent between the before and after situations. This can be written as

$$U(g_{ij}^0, g, M^0) = U(g_{ij}^1, g, M^0 + C).$$ (9.3)

where C = compensating variation.

The second measure is the equivalent variation. This is given by E in equation (9.4):

$$U(g_{ij}^1, g, M^0) = U(g_{ij}^0, g, M^0 + E).$$ (9.4)

We can readily compare thse two income-variation concepts with the consumers' surplus measure using the Marshallian form of demand function of the kind shown in Figure 9.2. The demand function relevant for defining the compensating variation is the compensated demand function, which is constructed on the assumption that real income is held constant as g_{ij} is altered. This is equivalent to saying, in Hicksian terms, that the consumer remains on the same indifference curve. The resulting change in consumption is termed the 'pure substitution effect.' The compensating variation is then the change in the area under the compensated demand function, shown by the area $g_{ij}^0 \, ad \, g_{ij}^1$ in Figure 9.2.

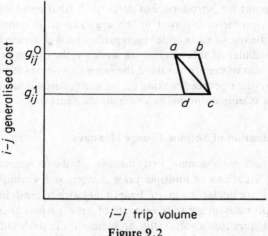

Figure 9.2

It should be emphasised that the path from point a to point d is a hypothetical one, unless the income effect for the good in question is zero. The actual path traced out, however, for a normal (that is non-inferior) good will be more like the path $a - c$ in Figure 9.2. As price falls, with money income constant, real income increases, and consumption of normal goods tends to increase with income. The measured consumers' surplus area, defined as the change in area under the actual demand function, will therefore tend to exceed the compensating variation (CV) measure of benefit.

The equivalent variation (EV) is obtained by moving back from g_{ij}^1 to g_{ij}^0 up the compensated demand function passing through point c, and is defined by the area $g_{ij}^0 bc g_{ij}^1$. Thus the measured consumers' surplus (CS) lies between the CV and EV measures with

$$\text{CV} \leqslant \Delta\text{CS} \leqslant \text{EV}$$

for the price-reduction case.

The validity of the consumers' surplus measure of benefit is related to the potential error involved in using it as an approximation for one or other of the income-variation concepts. Clearly, in this sense, the validity depends upon the size of the income effect associated with the good in question. The widespread use of the consumers' surplus measure in urban transport appraisal therefore rests upon a judgement that the income effects of the cost or price changes which occur are close to zero. The validity of this assumption has not yet been seriously challenged.

At this point we introduce, but defer for further consideration until Chapter 11, problems involved in the aggregation of individuals' surpluses and the use of areas under aggregate or market demand functions. For the remainder of this chapter we work on the operational assumption that a unit of benefit is valued the same to whoever it accrues. The analysis may then proceed making use of aggregative demand and benefit measures as simple summations of individual measures.

The Generalisation of Surplus-Change Measures

In this section we examine first the use of the consumers' surplus measure in situations of multiple price change, and second the extent to which a particular form of benefit algorithm used in transport evaluation provides an accurate estimate of 'true' surplus changes.

The first question involves the problem of the path independency of the benefit measure.[3] It will be recalled that the use of the consumers' surplus change measure involves the estimation of the change in area under a demand function following a change in the own price of a product. All other prices and money income are assumed constant. The estimation of the consumers' surplus change for a set of simultaneous price changes involves, conceptually at least, breaking down the total change into an ordered sequence of individual price changes. The total surplus change is then the sum of these individual surplus changes. The question arises of whether the value of the surplus change is independent of the sequence in which prices are altered.

Taking the simplest two-good case, we start with a price set (p_i^0, p_j^0) and consider the effects of two alternative paths to the new price set (p_i^1, p_j^1). The first is to take the path $(p_i^0, p_j^0) \rightarrow (p_i^1, p_j^0) \rightarrow (p_i^1, p_j^1)$. The alternative path is $(p_i^0, p_j^0) \rightarrow (p_i^0, p_j^1) \rightarrow (p_i^1, p_j^1)$.

The benefit measure on the first path is

$$B_1 = -\int_{p_i^0}^{p_i^1} f_i(p_i, p_j^0, M^0)\, dp_i - \int_{p_j^0}^{p_j^1} f_j(p_i^1, p_j, M^0)\, dp_j. \quad (9.5)$$

On the second it is

$$B_2 = -\int_{p_j^0}^{p_j^1} f_j\,(p_i^0, p_j, M^0)\,dp_j - \int_{p_i^0}^{p_i^1} f_i\,(p_i, p_j^1, M^0)\,dp_i. \qquad (9.6)$$

If we assume that the relevant functions, f_i and f_j, are linear in respect of cross-price effects then the condition for $B_1 = B_2$ is that

$$-\int_{p_j^0}^{p_j^1} \alpha_{ji}\, p_i\, dp_j = -\int_{p_i^0}^{p_i^1} \alpha_{ij}\, p_j\, dp_i, \qquad (9.7)$$

where

$$\alpha_{ij,ji} = \frac{\partial x_{ij}}{\partial p_{j,i}}, \text{ so that}$$

$$\alpha_{ji} = \alpha_{ij}. \qquad (9.8)$$

Thus path independence requires equality of cross-price effects, a result first noted in a classic paper by Hotelling.[4] It has also been noted, for example by Foster and Neuburger,[5] that this result requires the income elasticities of demand for i and j to be equal. They suggest that, whilst this is a restrictive condition, its infringement is unlikely to seriously bias results in practical evaluation problems.

The particular form of benefit algorithm used in transport-sector evaluation was first developed during the later stages of the London Transportation Study and is known as the L.T.S. method. The L.T.S. method expresses benefits for each $i-j$ zone pair as

$$\tfrac{1}{2}\,(t_{ij}^0 + t_{ij}^1)\,(g_{ij}^1 - g_{ij}^0). \qquad (9.9)$$

Total benefits are then the sum of (9.9) across all $i-j$ pairs. Thus in Figure 9.3 the L.T.S. method gives benefits equal to the area $ACEF + A^1C^1E^1F^1$. Sequential evaluation of consumers' surplus changes, by contrast, gives $ACDF + A^1B^1E^1F^1$ or $ABEF + A^1C^1D^1F^1$. If we assume that the relevant cross-effects are linear, or more generally the relevant cross-partial effects are equal, then the benefit using the L.T.S. method is equal to the benefit estimated by the sequential method if the demand functions are linear in own price.

This linearity assumption is a strong one, but it has great computational convenience. It also seems likely to produce estimates of acceptable accuracy in the urban transport context. The potential order of magnitude of error may be seen in the following way. If the individual's utility, U, is a function of prices, p, and income, M, then the change

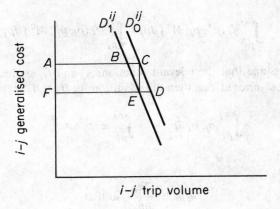

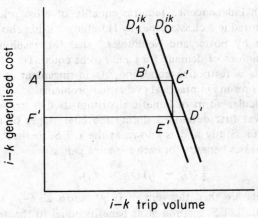

Figure 9.3

in utility consequent on a change in prices with M constant can be written

$$\Delta U = \sum_i U_i \, dp_i + \frac{1}{2} \sum_i \sum_j U_{ij} \, dp_i \, dp_j + \frac{1}{6} \sum_i \sum_j \sum_k U_{ijk} \, dp_i \, dp_j \, dp_k, \text{ etc. (9.10)}$$

where $U_i = \partial U_i / \partial P_i$.

Using the apparatus of conventional demand analysis, we know that if the individual maximises utility subject to his budget constraint, then the first-order conditions for a maximum are as follows:

$$U_i = - \lambda x_i \text{ for all } i \qquad (9.11)$$

and

$$M = \sum_i p_i x_i. \qquad (9.12)$$

λ, the undetermined multiplier attached to the budget constraint, is interpreted as the marginal utility of money. Using these results, the expression for ΔU can be rewritten as

$$\Delta U = - \sum_i x_i \, dp_i - \tfrac{1}{2} \sum_i \sum_j \frac{\partial x_i}{\partial p_j} \, dp_j \, dp_i + \sum_i \sum_j x_i \frac{\partial \lambda}{\partial p_j} \, dp_i \, dp_j, \text{ etc. } (9.13)$$

Noting that, with M constant,

$$dx_i = \sum_j \frac{\partial x_i}{\partial p_j} \, dp_j$$

(9.13) can be further simplified to

$$\Delta U = - \lambda \left\{ \sum_i x_i \, dp_i + \tfrac{1}{2} \sum_i dx_i \, dp_i, \text{ etc.} \ldots \right\} \qquad (9.14)$$

If we can assume that λ is approximately constant for the change of prices in question, then we can see that the monetary measure of welfare change involves terms in the observed prices and outputs. The linearity assumption involves a truncation of the expansion of ΔU after the second term. However, it is likely in most cases that the first term, shown in Figure 9.4 by the area $ABDE$, $\sum_i x_i \, dp_i$, will be the predominant one. The second term, $\tfrac{1}{2} dx_i \, dp_i$, gives the triangular area BCD in Figure 9.4. The approximation involved in the linearity assumption therefore extends no further than the error in taking the triangular measure. Some potential orders of magnitude of this error have been estimated by Reaume,[6] who found that the linear approximation of benefit did not diverge by more than 5 - 10 per cent from the 'true' benefit when the latter was estimated using up to third-order terms in the expansion. It is most unlikely that errors of this order are at all significant given the degree of approximation involved throughout the appraisal process as it has been described.

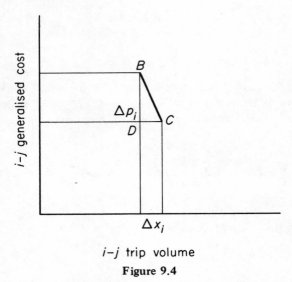

i–j trip volume

Figure 9.4

Application of the Surplus-Change Measures to Transport-Sector Evaluation — Cost Misperception

A straightforward application of the L.T.S. formula (9.9) gives transport-sector benefits a change in system costs (aggregated over all zone pairs, $i-j$, and modes, k) as

$$\sum_i \sum_j \sum_k \tfrac{1}{2} (t^0_{ijk} + t^1_{ijk}) (c^0_{ijk} - c^1_{ijk}). \tag{9.16}$$

Whilst this expression forms the basis of the benefit algorithm used in transport-sector evaluation, it must be extended to take account, first, of the misperception of the costs of car use, second, of changes in operators' surplus, and third, of changes in tax revenues of central government associated with switches in expenditure patterns. We deal with each of these points in turn.

The earlier discussion, for example in Chapter 5, has presented empirical evidence to support the contention that private-car users do not perceive the full marginal private costs involved in vehicle use. It was suggested that, at the most, the costs on which decision were based, in the absence of parking charges, were marginal fuel costs. If the car mode costs in equation (9.16) are treated as the perceived costs of car use, it follows that the consumers' surplus change relates to the change in perceived costs. However, this perceived surplus change is no longer a sufficient measure of individual welfare changes. A fuller estimate of the welfare change may be derived in the following way.

It has been suggested by Neuburger that a consumer's total expenditure, Y, may be disaggregated into two elements.[7] The first of these, O, may be termed an 'overheads' and 'contingencies' item. The overheads element would include items such as fixed charges for electricity or car insurance which have to be incurred in order for other consumption activities to be undertaken. The contingencies element covers items whose incidence either cannot be certainly predicted or which cannot be readily attributed to small changes in consumption behaviour. Items such as car repairs, or mileage-related depreciation, would fall into this category. It is assumed that the overheads and contingencies item takes first call on the consumer's budget. The balance, M, is then treated as the conventional budget constraint subject to which the individual seeks to maximise utility given a set of perceived costs. The basis for the division between M and O is not precisely specified. Thus, if p_i is the perceived cost of i, then

$$\sum_i p_i x_i = M. \tag{9.17}$$

Now, consider an item for which the full variable cost, f_i, exceeds the perceived cost, p_i. In this case part of the O expenditures is equal to

$$x_i (f_i - p_i). \tag{9.18}$$

The change in overheads and contingencies which results from a change in consumption, consequent on a change in p_i, can be written

$$dO = x_i^1 (f_i^1 - p_i^1) - x_i^0 (f_i^0 - p_i^0). \tag{9.19}$$

With Y constant and O taking first call on Y, M must change by an amount equal and opposite in sign to dO. With prices constant and assuming constancy of the marginal utility of income over the relevant range, the expression for the change in welfare resulting from the change in budget constraint can be written as

$$dU = \sum_i \frac{\partial U}{\partial x_i} dx_i$$

$$= \lambda \sum_i p_i dx_i. \tag{9.20}$$

The monetary measure of welfare change can then be written as

$$\frac{du}{\lambda} = \sum_i p_i dx_i = dM. \tag{9.21}$$

Thus the benefit expression embodied in equation (9.16) can be expanded to take account of cost misperception as follows:

$$\sum_i \sum_j \sum_k \frac{1}{2}(t^0_{ijk} + t^1_{ijk})(p^1_{ijk} - p^0_{ijk}) - \sum_i \sum_j \sum_k (t^1_{ijk}(f^1_{ijk} - p^1_{ijk})$$

$$- t^0_{ijk}(f^0_{ijk} - p^0_{ijk})), \tag{9.22}$$

where p_{ijk} = perceived cost of $i-j$ travel by mode k, and f_{ijk} = full private cost of $i-j$ travel by mode k.

In general for non-private-car modes, $p_{ijk} = f_{ijk}$, so the benefit expression reduces to the first term in (9.22).

Operators' Surplus

The 'pure' producers' surplus concept refers to the rents earned by intra-marginal factors of production when the factor-supply function is less than perfectly elastic. In principle, therefore, estimation of the total social surplus change should include any changes in intra-marginal rents which stem from the project or policy under consideration. To do so would involve the specification of the relevant factor-supply functions, not at all an easy matter. To date therefore the cost – benefit analysis of transport-sector projects has limited itself to include only changes in the surpluses accruing to operators in the form of the difference between fare income and variable operating costs. This can be taken as a reasonable approximation to the full producers' surplus measure if it is assumed that the changes in surpluses accruing to other factors stemming from the change under consideration are second order. It is a more exact measure still if it is assumed that these factors are in perfectly elastic supply to the individual operator over the relevant range of output changes.

The two activities for which changes in producers' surplus are potentially significant in the transport sector are public transport and parking operation. We illustrate the argument using the public-transport case. Change in operators' surplus can be estimated as the difference between the change in fare revenues and the change in vehicle operating costs for the public-transport system between the base and 'do-something' situations. Because it is usually impossible to attribute public-transport operating costs to particular trips, the estimation of operators' surplus is usually done on a system-wide basis. Thus if R^0 is fare revenue and C^0 the system operating costs in the before situation, and R^1 and C^1 the same items in the after situation, operators' surplus change is simply

$$(R^1 - C^1) - (R^0 - C^0) = \Delta R - \Delta C. \tag{9.23}$$

This term must be added to the expanded users' benefit term given by equation (9.22).

Indirect Taxes

If the average rate of indirect taxation in the transport and non-transport sectors of the economy were uniform, then switches in expenditure between one sector and another would leave the total indirect tax take unchanged. The benefit expression in (9.22), supplemented by equation (9.23), would then stand as a full statement of benefits if it could also be assumed that prices of non-transport-sector outputs remained unchanged.[8]

However, average indirect tax rates in the transport sector are not equal to those outside, and within transport itself there are quite wide divergences, for example between private-car use and public transport. Because this is the case, switches in expenditure between the transport and non-transport sectors involve changes in tax revenues; since these are akin to producers' surpluses, account must be taken of them in the evaluation process.

The total change in indirect taxes across the economy is the sum of changes within the transport sector and in the rest of the economy. The procedure for estimating the benefit change may be illustrated by taking a simple two-sector model of the economy, with a transport sector, T, and a non-transport sector, N. Then let t_T = the average indirect (value-added) tax rate in the transport sector, t_N = the average indirect (value-added) tax rate in the non-transport sector. Total consumers' expenditure, E, is equal to

$$E_T + E_N. \qquad (9.24)$$

Total indirect tax revenue in the before situation is then

$$E_T^0 \phi_T + E_N^0 \phi_N, \qquad (9.25)$$

where

$$\phi_{T,N} = \frac{t_{T,N}}{1 + t_{T,N}}.$$

In the after situation tax revenue equals

$$E_T^1 \phi_T + E_N^1 \phi_N. \qquad (9.26)$$

We assume that ϕ_T and ϕ_N are constant, and that total expenditure, E, is constant. It follows that

$$\Delta T = \phi_T \Delta E_T + \phi_N \Delta E_N$$

$$= \Delta E_T (\phi_T - \phi_N) \text{ since } \Delta E_T = -\Delta E_N.$$

$$(9.27)$$

Conventional practice has been to combine the 'within-transport' change with the cost-misperception term,[9] noting that

$$f_i = r_i + i_i, \tag{9.28}$$

where i_i = indirect tax, and r_i = resource cost of i. The total change in indirect taxes in the transport sector is equal to

$$\sum_i \sum_j \sum_k (t^1_{ijk} i_{ijk} - t^0_{ijk} i_{ijk}). \tag{9.29}$$

Combining this with the misperception term in equation (9.22) gives

$$\sum_i \sum_j \sum_k \left\{ t^0_{ijk} (r^0_{ijk} - p^0_{ijk}) - t^1_{ijk} (r^1_{ijk} - p^1_{ijk}) \right\}. \tag{9.30}$$

The change in tax in the non-transport sector is then

$$-\Delta E_T \phi_N. \tag{9.31}$$

The conventional benefit measure is then the sum of expressions (9.16), (9.30) and (9.31), with $c_{ijk} = p_{ijk}$ in (9.16).

However, it can be argued that this conventional treatment 'under-values' the change in tax revenue given by (9.27) above. The literature

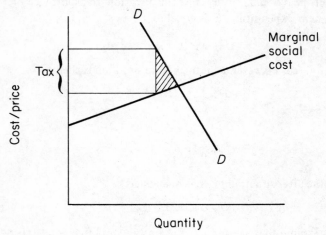

Figure 9.5

on optimal taxation suggests that the shadow price of tax revenue is greater than unity.[10] This follows because commodity taxes involve a 'deadweight' loss to society shown by the shaded triangular area in Figure 9.5, representing the difference between marginal social cost and the demand function. This line of argument therefore suggests that increments to tax resulting from expenditure switching should be valued more highly than is done in the conventional method.

The Benefit in the Fixed Trip Matrix Case

It is assumed in conventional urban transport modelling that certain kinds of trip are not sensitive in the origin – destination pattern to changes in transport system costs, although they may be sensitive in respect of choice of route. The most important categories of trip for which this assumption is made are, first, commercial vehicle trips, and second, through journeys, whether commercial vehicles or person trips (that is journeys with both origin and destination outside the area being studied).

In this case the benefit expression reduces to the change in resource costs for the fixed volume of trips between each $i - j$ pair, irrespective of whether there is cost misperception or not. If there is no misperception, then the transport-sector benefits are

$$\sum_i \sum_j t_{ij} \left(f_{ij}^0 - f_{ij}^1\right) + \sum_i \sum_j t_{ij} \left(i_{ij}^1 - i_{ij}^0\right) = \sum_i \sum_j t_{ij} \left(r_{ij}^0 - r_{ij}^1\right). \quad (9.32)$$

If there is misperception, then the benefit expression becomes

$$\sum_i \sum_j t_{ij} \left(p_{ij}^0 - p_{ij}^1\right) - \sum_i \sum_j t_{ij} \left\{\left(f_{ij}^1 - p_{ij}^1\right) - \left(f_{ij}^0 - p_{ij}^0\right)\right\} + \sum_i \sum_j t_{ij} \left(i_{ij}^1 - i_{ij}^0\right)$$

$$= \sum_i \sum_j t_{ij} \left(r_{ij}^0 - r_{ij}^1\right). \quad (9.33)$$

Conclusion

It may be noted that for presentational purposes the over-all benefit measure can be disaggregated by types of benefit, although these types of benefit should not be taken as a final measure of incidence (this point is taken up in Chapter 11). Using the planning balance sheet approach developed by Lichfield,[11] benefits might be disaggregated into the following:

(1) Users' benefits – given by equations (9.22) and (9.32/9.33);
(2) Operators' surplus changes – equation (9.23); and
(3) Government – equation (9.27).

This chapter has shown how a benefit expression for use in transport-sector evaluation may be derived from a more general benefit expression based on the Marshallian consumers' surplus concept.

The following chapter discusses problems in the aggregation of benefits and the criteria by which projects or policies are assessed.

CHAPTER TEN

Evaluation Criteria and their Implications for Benefit Estimation

The Evaluation Criterion

In the idealised evaluation procedure set out in Chapter 1, it was assumed that the end-product of the forecasting and benefit estimation process would be a project benefit profile. When transformed to present-value terms by the appropriate set of discount factors, this would then be compared with the present value of the capital costs of the project. The outcome of the evaluation would depend upon the context in which it was undertaken. The two most significant variable factors here are, first, whether there is some mutually exclusive alternative to the project under consideration by the sponsoring organisation, and second, whether the capital-expenditure budget of the organisation is or is not subject to an upper limit. The appropriate criterion under each of the four alternative outcomes generated by the two variable factors is shown in Table 10.1. ΔNPV refers to the incremental net present value (N.P.V.) over the alternative project. r is equal to the marginal benefit - cost ratio for the investment programme as a whole.

TABLE   10.1

		Capital budget constraint	
		No 1	Yes 2
Mutually exclusive projects	No	$\mathrm{NPV} > 0$	$\dfrac{\mathrm{NPV}}{C} > r$
		3	4
	Yes	$\mathrm{NPV} > 0$	$\dfrac{\Delta \mathrm{NPV}}{\Delta C} > r$

Various more complex schemes can of course be devised. In particular, even in the simplest case, a positive N.P.V. to construction in year 0 may not be sufficient justification for starting the project immediately. A further condition, that the first-year return should exceed the discount rate, is often imposed in cases where the benefit stream is time dependent.[1]

A comparison of this planning paradigm with the form of evaluation procedure actually undertaken in many recent U.K. urban transportation studies is instructive. We start by briefly noting some of the main features of the process. (It should be noted that whilst this stands as an account of general tendencies it is not necessarily an accurate description of procedures in any particular study.)

First, the studies have generally been directed towards the 'best' way of spending an exogenously given planning budget.[2] It is assumed that this budget will be spent by the time of the study design year, usually ten to fifteen years forward, but the budget is usually not expressed in present-value terms, implying indifference to the actual pattern of expenditure up to the design year.

Second, the studies usually examine a small number of alternative strategies. In the first round of major conurbation studies the alternative strategies usually embodied different mixes of highway and public-transport infrastructure expenditure. Option choice in these circumstances can be represented in terms of Figure 10.1. *I* represents an iso-

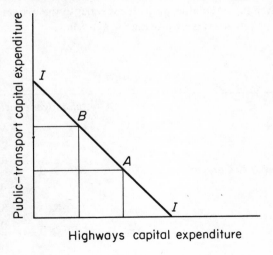

Figure 10.1

expenditure line and the axes indicate levels of public-transport and highway infrastructure expenditure. Point A would represent a highway orientated option, point B a public-transport orientated option.

More recently the scope of studies has been expanded to allow the examination of options involving revenue support for public transport, so that the expenditure constraint refers both to capital and specified current items. Conversely, surpluses on parking operations are allowed to offset expenditures. Whilst noting that the implications of extending the scope of studies in this way greatly increases the difficulty of interpreting their results,[3] we ignore the potential complications in the discussion which follows.

Third, the alternative options are usually compared with an option called a 'do-nothing, do-minimum or economic-base option'. In each case therefore the (p^0) price set refers to the level of costs or prices produced by the interaction of demand and supply in the economic base. In the case of highway networks this economic base typically embodies only those schemes or projects which are highly committed (in practice, the definition of 'committed' is often somewhat flexible and open to negotiation). On the public-transport side the 'do-nothing' concept is more difficult to define. Trends in many U.K. urban areas have been for increasing real fares, reduced service levels and declining public-transport patronage; until recently therefore practice has been to assume, broadly speaking, a continuation of these trends up to the design year. Some local authorities have recently taken steps to arrest this decline by a variety of measures, and in some cases appear to have had some success (albeit sometimes at the cost of rapidly mounting operating deficits). In these conditions, the economic base might be more appropriately defined in terms of the position given certain continuing policies.

Finally, the standard criterion on which options have been compared is the design-year rate of return, defined as the ratio of estimated design-year benefits to the (approximately constant across options) level of expenditure. The expenditure figure is usually undiscounted.

Two questions may be asked of the appraisal criterion: First, accepting that the studies have been in the business of determining the best way of spending a predetermined budget, how efficient is the design-year return (or design-year benefit) as a means of ranking alternatives? Second, whatever the exact nature of the appraisal exercise, we want to know something about 'value-for-money' in the absolute sense. It can be argued that if we were not interested at all in the admissibility problem, then in many cases we would not even go to the bother of producing an estimate of annual benefits. If, for example, the modelling process produced benefit estimates for 'representative' peak and off-peak hours, alternatives could be ranked on the basis alone, so long as one alternative was superior in respect both of peak and off-peak periods. Even if one alternative was not 'dominant', it would be sufficient to rank on the basis of estimated 'representative' daily not annual benefits. We therefore wish to know whether any useful indicators of admissibility can be derived from a design-year rate of return figure.

With regard to project ranking, our criterion for efficiency is whether the ranking produced by the design-year return is the same as the one that would be produced by a full present-value appraisal. The maximand in the present-value case will be

$$P(B)_i - P(C)_i, \tag{10.1}$$

where $P(B)_i$ = present value of benefits of option i, and $P(C)_i$ = present value of capital costs of option i. Thus in the case where we are choosing between two alternatives, x and y, we wish to know whether

$$\frac{B(t)x}{C_x} > \frac{B(t)y}{C_y} \tag{10.2}$$

implies

$$P(B)_x - P(C)_x > P(B)_y - P(C)_y. \tag{10.3}$$

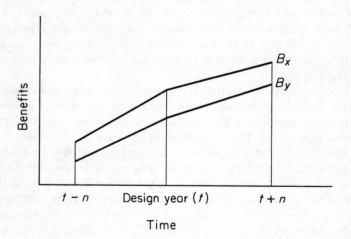

Figure 10.2

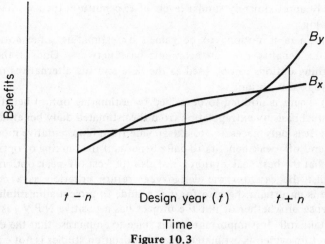

Time

Figure 10.3

The design-year procedure gives us a snapshot at a point in time of an over-all benefit profile. There is, in general, nothing that we can say of an *a priori* nature about whether the profiles of x and y will be 'well-behaved' with respect to their design-year value, as in Figure 10.2, or whether we have a situation like that shown in Figure 10.3 where $P(B)_y$ may well exceed $P(B)_x$. We may note that for any option i we can write

$$P(B)_i = a_i B(n)_i \qquad (10.4)$$

All we can say is that if options are 'of a kind' with one another, then a_i, which is a function of benefit growth rates on either side of the design year, is unlikely to differ greatly from one option to another.

The same argument applies on the capital-costs side. The present value of capital expenditures can be written as some function, f_i, of cumulative expenditures up to the design year, c_i. In principle more information is available about capital-expenditure profiles since the implementation of a strategy may imply a definite sequence of expenditures on individual terms. However, we cannot say *a priori* whether the expenditure pattern which emerges will be roughly the same for each strategy.

Our conclusion on the question of the validity of the design-year return as a ranking device is therefore an agnostic one. In certain cases it may be valid, in others it may not. We note, however, that if the object of the exercise is simply to rank options, and if these options embody approximately similar levels of expenditure, then we have the following.

(1) There is nothing to be gained by estimating some notion of absolute benefits over an economic-base network. One of the do-something options can be used as the base and the alternatives ranked relative to this option.

(2) There is nothing to be gained by estimating option benefits on an annual basis by extrapolation from the estimated daily benefits.

(3) It is only necessary to extrapolate from representative modelled peak and off-peak benefits to daily benefits if the ranking of options is such that the best peak option is not also the best off-peak option.

Whilst the case for the design-year return criterion as a ranking device is uncertain, the case for it as a guide to project admissibility (in the sense of whether or not the project has a positive N.P.V.) is more uncertain still. It is important at this stage to emphasise that the design-year return which is estimated for transportation studies is not equivalent to the so-called 'first-year rate of return' which often serves an an indicator of the appropriate construction date for a project. In the simpler cases, where the project gestation period is relatively short, and the project itself is relatively long lived, then the estimated first-year return may be a good guide to project admissibility.

To see this we write the first-year return for construction in time period $t - 1$ as

$$\frac{B(t)}{C(t - 1)} = r. \tag{10.5}$$

Let the benefit function be time dependent, and let

$$B(u) > 0. \tag{10.6}$$

For example, let $B(u) = B_t e^{g(u - t)}$ (exponential benefits growth). Then, if $t = 1$, the project present value may be written as

$$P = B_1 \int_1^\infty e^{-mu}\, du - C, \tag{10.7}$$

where $m = g - i$, and i = the discount rate.

The upper limit of the benefit integral is taken to infinity for simplicity. If

$$\frac{B_1}{C} = i, \tag{10.8}$$

then (10.7) can be written as

$$P = C_i \int_1^\infty e^{-mu} \, du - C$$

$$= \frac{C_i}{m} [e^{-m}] - C. \tag{10.9}$$

Present value is positive if

$$C_i (e^{-m}) > C_m, \tag{10.10}$$

with (1) $i > m$, (2) small m. Then it can be seen that the first-year return may be a good guide to admissibility. The design-year return, unfortunately, does not have this desirable property, since its transformation into a present value requires information both about the benefit profile before and after the design year, and the capital expenditure profile. That is to say, the present value of the option tested on the basic of a design-year, n, may be written as

$$\sum_{t=0}^{t=n-1} B_t (1+i)^{-t} + \sum_{t=n}^{t=n+x} B_t (1+i)^{-t} - \sum_{t=0}^{t=n-1} C_t (1+i)^{-t}. \tag{10.11}$$

The two benefit summations will be quite unrelated since benefit changes in the pre-design-year period will be related both to factors generating benefit change over time, and to the level of accumulated capital expenditure embodied in completed projects.

We conclude that the design-year return in itself provides little or no guidance about project admissibility. As in the context of project ranking, however, it is true that if assumptions are made about the nature of the capital expenditure and benefit profiles, then an estimate of present value can be made using the design-year benefit estimate as, so to speak, a pivot. But it should be emphasised that such an estimate would be no more than an informed guess in the absence of any empirical information on the behaviour of project benefits over time. Information of this kind can only be obtained by undertaking further modelling embodying demand estimates for a year or years other than the design year, so that interpolation can be attempted between the two (or more) observed points of the benefit function.

At this point we note that the factors affecting the level of estimated benefits are complex, arising both from changes in the level of demand for travel, and from changes in the values of parameters in the generalised cost function, in particular the value of travel time.

The fact that studies have continued to utilise a criterion which is manifestly unsatisfactory both as a guide to the ranking of alternatives and to admissibility is due largely to the potentially heavy costs involved in extending the benefit estimation process from a single to a multi-year basis. In addition, however, it can be argued that it reflects upon the relatively marginal status of economic evaluation procedures in the over all appraisal process. It should be emphasised that this marginal status reflects a proper scepticism of the real uncertainties involved in any appraisal process.

The Derivation of Daily and Annual Benefits

Whatever one's scepticism about the present role of economic evaluation procedures in the over-all process of appraising alternatives, it is clear that progress on this front should lie in the direction of extending benefit estimation procedures to cover more than the design year. However, if this is done then there are still difficulties in extrapolating the benefits estimated in respect of representative weekday peak and off-peak hours to produce an estimate of annual benefits. We briefly consider this problem before turning, in the next chapter, to a discussion of some more general problems of economic evaluation.

The simplest and most obvious procedure for the estimation of daily benefits is to take the estimate of benefits in a peak hour and then to factor this by

$$\frac{\sum_i T_i}{T_{\text{PEAK}}} \, ,$$

where $\sum_i T_i$ is equal to the total daily volume of trips and T_{PEAK} is the volume of trips made in the peak hour. Total weekly benefits could then be estimated by applying a further factor, reflecting the ratio of total weekly trip volumes to the trip volume of the representative weekday.

A procedure of this kind implies a simple proportionate relationship between trip volumes and benefits of the following kind:

$$B_i = KT_i, \tag{10.12}$$

where B_i = benefits in time period i, and T_i = trips in time period i.

An alternative procedure would be to estimate benefits in a peak and an off-peak hour. If it is also assumed that the benefit function passes through the origin, then a 'curve' might be fitted to the three points as shown in Figure 10.4. As drawn, the relationship is non-linear. In this

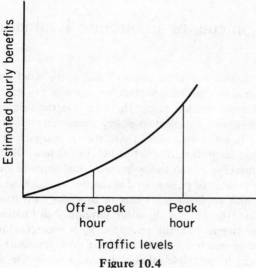

Figure 10.4

case, the total estimated benefits are not independent of the distribution of hourly trip volumes, and a further procedure must then be specified for obtaining this distribution.

Exactly the same problems apply in moving from the benefits estimated for the representative weekday to annual benefits. All of this is bound to be a somewhat approximate process. It is in this light that the remarks made in Chapter 9 about the use of the linear approximation to demand functions should be viewed.

CHAPTER ELEVEN

Some Problems in Economic Evaluation

The benefit measures used in conventional cost - benefit analysis and applied within the urban transport sector appraisal process are based on hypothetical compensation tests. These involve the summation of the costs and benefits of a project or policy irrespective of to whom they accrue. If the benefits exceed the costs, then it is argued that society as a whole would be potentially better off, in the sense that the gainers could compensate losers so that everyone could be made better off as a result of the project or policy. In this chapter we examine a number of problems in the application of this methodology in urban transport appraisal. First, the benefit algorithm developed in Chapter 9 covered only the 'movement' benefits produced by a project. However, there are a number of external effects associated with transport projects and policies which, in principle, should be included in the cost - benefit analysis. These external effects fall largely under the environmental heading, and in the first section of the chapter we discuss the incorporation of these effects into the cost-benefit framework. Second, certain objections have been raised to the form of compensation test described above. The relevance of these in transport-sector evaluation is considered in the second section. The third section of the chapter examines the problem of specifying the projects and policies to be assessed. The final section examines the estimation of benefits when a new mode or service is introduced.

Environmental Evaluation

The objective of environmental evaluation procedures is to incorporate certain external effects of transport projects into the cost - benefit analysis of these projects.

The concept of external effects, or spillovers, may be defined in terms of the production function of the firm in the following way.[1] In the absence of external effects, the production function for firm i takes the following form:

$$q_i = f(x_{i1}, \ldots, x_{in}), \tag{11.1}$$

where q_i = quantity produced by firm i, x_{i1} 1, ..., x_{in} = firm i's inputs of factors 1 ... n. If externalities are present, the production function for firm i takes the following form:

$$q_i = f(x_i, ..., x_{in}; q_j), \qquad (11.2)$$

where q_j = firm j's output. External effects can equally well be expressed in terms of individual utility functions. In the absence of external effects, the arguments of the utility function refer only to the individual's own consumption of goods and services. However, in the presence of externalities, the function takes the following form:

$$U_i = f(x_{i1}, ..., x_{in}; x_{jk}), \qquad (11.3)$$

where x_{i1}, ..., x_{in} = i's consumption of goods 1 ... n, x_{jk} = j's consumption of good k. External diseconomies occur when

$$\frac{\partial u_i}{\partial x_{jk}} < 0$$

and

$$x_{jk} > 0. \qquad (11.4)$$

An obvious example of an external diseconomy in the transport sector is when x_{jk} represents j's use of a particular piece of road space on to which i's house fronts. The source of diseconomy in this case is the nuisance imposed on i by j.

Transport generates a number of external effects on the environment. Attention in the United Kingdom has largely been confined to the diseconomies imposed in the form of noise and visual intrusion, although more recently increasing emphasis has been given to problems of pedestrian – vehicle conflict and severance. The concepts of noise and pedestrian – vehicle conflict are self-explanatory. Visual intrusion refers to the impact either of physical structures or vehicles on the field of vision of an observer located in an adjacent property. Severance refers to the impact of transport structures on the pedestrian connectivity of particular communities.

The full incorporation of environmental effects into an economic evaluation process involves both the estimation of the physical impact of projects or policies and the conversion of whatever physical measure is used into monetary units. Because physical measurement and forecasting problems have been fully dealt with elsewhere,[2] attention is focused on the conversion of physical impact measures into monetary terms.

The most widely used approach to the problem of converting physical into monetary measures has been to examine possible trade-off situations in which people have the opportunity to incur additional expenditure in order to achieve a more favourable environment. One area of investigation which has seemed particularly promising in this respect has been residential property values. The idea here is to estimate a relationship between property values and a set of explanatory variables which include environmental variables such as differences in average noise levels. The regression coefficient of the 'noise' variable may then be interpreted as the capitalised present value of differences in noise levels.

There are certain statistical problems with this approach. The first arises through possible multi-collinearity between the explanatory variables. For example, we would expect, *ceteris paribus,* that property values would be positively related to accessibility, and negatively related to noise level. But highly accessible properties such as those adjacent to main bus routes might also be relatively noisy. A second type of problem arises if the relationship between property value and noise is itself non-linear as shown in Figure 11.1. Clearly, the change in property values per unit change in noise level is very different over the two ranges of the noise variable shown in Figure 11.1. Empirical work should therefore aim to utilise observations with a sufficiently wide

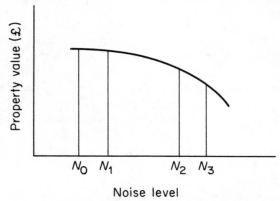

Figure 11.1 The relationship between property values and noise levels (hypothetical)

spread of observed noise levels. Furthermore, if the average noise level was increasing over time, then observations would more and more be grouped around the relatively flat portion of the curve. The general deterioration in the noise climate might then prevent people's preferences from being properly observable.

Another approach to the valuation of noise might be to examine people's willingness to undertake noise-reducing expenditure such as double-glazed windows. The problem here is one of joint products. Double-glazing may purchase not only noise reduction but also reduction in heating bills. It is not obvious how the valuation placed on each of the joint products can be separately identified.

From this discussion we can see that there are substantial problems to be overcome before the effects of varying noise levels can be converted into monetary units. The same is also true of the other dimensions of environmental effect described earlier. This inability to convert physical measures of environmental effect into monetary units produces an obvious problem of how information on environmental effects can be related to movement benefits expressed in monetary terms.

The first and most straightforward approach is to present the different elements of the over-all assessment as they are. Thus traffic benefits of alternatives would be expressed in monetary units, and the environmental aspects would be expressed in terms of the relevant physical measure. One way of presenting information on environmental factors is in the form of an environmental-impact statement. This sets out, for example, the number of people exposed to different levels of noise or visual intrusion under each alternative being considered. This approach emphasises the distribution of noise levels rather than the average level. This would seem to be justified by the experience of some recent U.K. transportation studies which have found that whilst the forecast average noise level throughout a study area varies relatively little between options, there may be significant differences in the distribution of noise levels.

The impact-statement approach is clearly useful as a presentational device. Of itself, however, this does not resolve the difficulty of choosing between alternatives, the ranking of which on environmental impact differs from that on measured benefits. If there is a single dimension to the environmental impact, then, in principle, the decision-maker can be presented with a relatively straightforward trade-off situation. Does he consider £ x of additional traffic benefit to be worth more than y units of environmental disbenefit? However, such simiplicity is perhaps misleading, because of the nature of physical measures used in environmental-impact analysis. A decibel is not a measure whose significance can be readily grasped.

Faced with this difficulty, there is a temptation for the analyst to ease the task of the ultimate decision-maker by expressing benefits in terms of some common unit rather than in the different units used in the traffic and environmental aspect of the evaluation. A variety of methods have been devised for doing this, such as the Goals Achievement Matrix. [3] The starting point here is to define certain goals and then to assess the performance of alternatives in achieving them. The temptation with an approach of this kind is to abandon the attempt to estimate costs and benefits in monetary terms, and to express everything in quantitative but non-monetary terms. If this is done, then each alternative can be ranked or scored in terms of whatever objectives have been set; weightings based either on the analyst's own preferences or those of some relevant group of people, such as local politicians, can be attached to each objective, and, by combining weights and scores, a single number or score can be produced for each alternative.

A procedure of this kind might have something to offer as a preliminary screening device, that is as a means of eliminating options with particularly adverse effects in certain directions. However, it is of no use whatsoever in considering admissibility problems, and it appears to be of little assistance in the final stages of evaluation, even when the alternatives involve approximately the same cost. Indeed, in so far as it discourages the measurement of costs and benefits in monetary terms, then it may be positively unhelpful.

A final alternative approach to integrating environmental effects into a cost–benefit framework is to define certain environmental standards and then to estimate the cost involved in meeting these standards for each of the alternatives under consideration. The measured benefits of each alternative would then be related to a level of costs which embodied whatever expenditure was necessary to achieve the environmental standards. It has sometimes been suggested that a procedure of this kind will tend to reduce the present value of 'do-something' alternatives. However, if 'environmental-correction' costs are expressed as increments over the level involved in achieving specified standards in the economic base, then it is not obvious that this need be the case. The required environmental standards can be expressed in a variety of ways. For example, limits can be set on admissible traffic-noise levels or on the extent of visual intrusion. Estimates can then be made of the cost of satisfying these constraints in some cost-minimising fashion.

The most obvious problem with this approach is the extent to which officially imposed standards reflect individuals' preferences. There are two opposite tendencies at work here. If the 'acceptable' noise standard is set at a decibels, then we might estimate that y properties will suffer noise levels greater than a. If double-glazing, cost c per dwelling, is the prescribed minimum-cost method of reducing noise levels, then the evaluation would attribute a cost of cy to the satisfaction of the environmental standard. However, we might observe currently, that only a proportion, p, of properties suffering from noise levels greater than x decibels actually bother to double-glaze. In this case, it might be argued that a better estimate of the cost would be pcy. However, the cost c will represent a minimum estimate of the benefit derived from double-glazing for those households which have actually installed double-glazing. We might also observe that the proportion of people undertaking double-glazing at any given noise levels was an increasing function of average household income. If this were the case, then the p value relevant in ten to fifteen years' time would be higher than today's p value on account of higher average household incomes. A final problem, to which we have already drawn attention, is that double-glazing may produce other benefits than noise reduction. It is not obvious how to attribute the costs associated with these joint products.

The Incorporation of Distributional Effects into Appraisal Procedures

Two sorts of objections arising from a concern for distribution matters have been voiced from time to time about the validity of hypothetical compensation tests as indicators of welfare change. The first and more obtuse difficulty arises in the case where the impact of the project or policy in question produces large changes either in relative prices or in the distribution of incomes. In this case, it is possible for a movement from one set of outputs to another to permit a potential welfare gain at the before set of relative prices, but for a reversion to the before output levels to allow a potential welfare gain at the after set of relative prices [4]. This is an interesting possibility. However, it is most unlikely that the projects and policies considered by the urban transport appraisal process will result in outcomes of this extreme nature.

There is a second objection to the hypothetical compensation tests based on unweighted costs and benefits. It is sometimes suggested that if a set of weights reflecting value judgements about the social utility of income to each individual was applied to project costs and benefits, then this weighted sum might be negative even if the unweighted sum was positive (and vice versa). This is sometimes thought to be a potentially serious problem in the urban transport sector. An example offered in support of this contention may be found in discussions of alternative ways of restraining private-car use in urban areas. Restraint may be achieved through the pricing mechanism, whether by direct road pricing, supplementary licensing or increased parking charges. It is argued that 'fiscal' measures of this kind will bear particularly heavily on relatively low-income car users, and that therefore restraint measures which rely on physical or administered methods are preferable. We do not propose to resolve the merits of this particular case; it is sufficient to note that there clearly is a problem here which can only be resolved by examining both the efficiency and distributional impacts of alternative restraint policies.

A slightly different concern which has been voiced recently involves the areal distribution of benefits from transport projects. For example, it has been suggested that the measured benefits of public-transport infrastructure investments which increase the accessibility of residential areas with relatively low average household incomes should by implication be adjusted upwards on income-distributional grounds. The underlying assumption here is that the 'movement' benefits of the transport improvement do actually accrue to the low-income residents. Whilst this may be true in terms of the 'first-round effect', it is quite possible that the ultimate incidence will be somewhat different; for example, housing rentals in the area of improved accessibility may be bid up. We can currently say very little of an empirical nature about the incidence of gains from the reduced transport costs, especially in urban areas. The potential difficulties involved in tracing through the incidence of project costs in policies involving additional expenditure either of a current or capital nature by the public authority concerned are even more severe. Because of this we need to be extremely cautious about the use of any simple tableau approach which attempts to distribute benefits and costs between groups such as 'road users' and the rest of society or between residents of one part of an area and another.

This discussion suggests that while there may be considerable uncertainties attaching to the value of the unweighted gains and losses from urban transport projects and policies, the uncertainties attaching to their ultimate incidence between different groups of people are far greater. Whilst it may be desirable to make whatever rough quantitative assessments one can about distributional impacts, the central focus of any piece of cost–benefit appraisal in the urban transport sector must be the presentation of the estimated unweighted costs and benefits.

The Specification of Projects or Policies

The evaluation procedure described in Chapter 9 seeks to measure benefits in terms of the changes in travel conditions and travel volumes which are predicted to occur if certain actions are undertaken. This involves careful specification of both the base, or do-nothing situation, and the do-something conditions so as to ensure that the benefits which are measured really are attributable to the particular do-something option being examined.

A frequently encountered problem in urban transport evaluation is that the base with which the do-something option is compared may embody certain kinds of operating inefficiency. The benefits which stem from any reduction of these inefficiencies which occurs as a by-product of a particular do-something option may then be credited to the project or policy under consideration. However, it is possible that their removal or reduction could be achieved in other ways. If this is the case then only the additional benefits which accrue over and above those resulting from whatever measures may be available to minimise inefficiency in the base situation should be credited to the project.

Two examples of the problem can be offered. The first occurs in the context of urban transportation studies.[5] Some of the do-something options examined in recent U.K. studies have included both infrastructure investment and restraint measures. The options are tested against a base which does not usually embody any significant degree of restraint. A simplified representation of this situation in terms of a single link in a transport network is shown in Figure 11.2. We assume for simplicity that the 'price' confronting the user in the do-something case is equal to the marginal social cost (*MSC*). In the before situation price is equal to average social cost (*ASC*). Benefits to the capacity expansion, given by the area *ABCD*, then include an element, shown by the area *BXE*, which represents a loss of benefits associated with non-optimal level of use in the before situation. However, if the transport authority had been able to eliminate this 'dead-loss' element in the before situation, by restraint measures which could be undertaken independently of the capacity expansion, then clearly benefits to the capacity expansion *per se* are overstated by *BXE*.

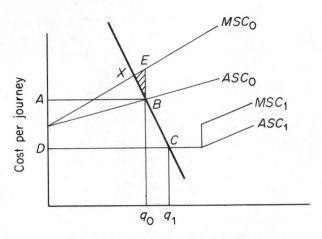

Traffic flow per hour

Figure 11.2

The second example concerns the estimation of the effects of restraint on private-car use on public-transport operations and finances. Any form of traffic restraint will generally result in the diversion of some peak-hour trips currently made by private car to public transport. However, if public-transport capacity in peak travel times is fully used, then additional costs will be incurred by the public-transport operator. If the marginal costs of providing additional peak-hour capacity are high, and if peak-hour fares do not currently reflect these costs, then the net benefit of introducing a restraint policy will be reduced and (perversely) the public-transport operator's finances weakened.

In some recent studies,[6] however, the predicted additional public-transport journeys made by people who switch from car as a result of restraint appear to be carried at little or no additional cost to the public transport operator. This implies either that the operating conditions for public transport improve to such an extent that the larger volume of trips can be carried by the same stock of vehicles and crews; or, alternatively, that the operator has spare capacity in the peak hour which can cater for the extra trips. It is not obvious that a mismatch of supply and demand of this kind on public transport requires the introduction of restraint measures to correct it. If the mismatching can be corrected by the operator independently of whatever restraint measures are undertaken, then it is clearly incorrect to attribute the benefits of filling spare capacity to restraint policies. The correct measure of the benefits of restraint would require an initial matching of public-transport supply and demand in the base. Any additional public-transport trips generated by restraint would then require additional capacity, except to the extent that effective capacity was increased through improved operating conditions. Alternatively, capacity might remain unchanged, in which case service quality would deteriorate. In the absence of peak pricing on public transport it is a moot point which of the options (to adjust or not to adjust capacity) would be the more efficient.

New Modes

This section discusses the application of the benefit alogithm developed in Chapter 9 to cases where either a service or mode is withdrawn or a new service or mode is introduced.

The most straightforward form of benefit algorithm set out in Chapter 9 for $i-j$ trips by mode k was

$$B_k = \tfrac{1}{2}(q^1_{ijk} + q^2{}_{ijk})(C^1_{ijk} - C^2_{ijk}), \tag{11.5}$$

where B_k = benefits to mode k, q^1_{ijk} = 'before' trips between i and j on mode k, q^2_{ijk} = 'after' trips between i and j on mode k, C^1_{ijk}, C^2_{ijk} = before/after costs between i and j on mode k. An expression of this kind is inapplicable in situations where either C^1_{ijk} or C^2_{ijk} is undefined due to the non-availability of mode k. In this case the consumers' surplus gain or loss of a service which is not available in either the before or after situation is given by the integral area under the demand function. The limits of integration are given between the generalised cost at which the mode or service is introduced, or withdrawn, and an upper limit cost at which demand tends to zero. This is shown by the area ABC in Figure 11.3.

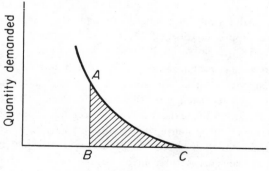

Generalised cost per journey

Figure 11.3

The practical difficulties of applying this methodology stem first from the potentially large number of integrations that may have to be performed, and second from the need to specify a demand function over an unusually wide range of generalised costs. Taking the first point, the evaluation of a new transit system serving only, say, twenty zones of an urban area would require the specification of up to 190 zone-to-zone demand relationships. Some of the difficulties involved in estimating the demand for new modes have already been discussed.

Taking the second point, the demand function for new or withdrawn modes or services is shown in Figure 11.4. The behaviour of this func-

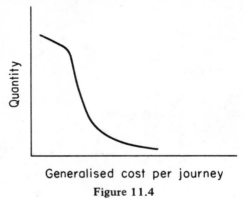

Generalised cost per journey

Figure 11.4

tion at relatively high generalised costs is extremely uncertain. There may therefore be merit in extending the linear approximation of the central part of the function to define an upper limit cost at which demand tends to zero. This is shown in Figure. 11.5. Alternatively, even simpler rules of thumb, such as 'upper limit cost equals k time cost at introduction/withdrawal', could be devised and the benefits estimated using a linear approximation of the demand function between thus upper limit and C_{ijk}^1.

A final problem in evaluating service introduction or withdrawal concerns the concept of option demand.[7] The general point here is that non-users of a facility, such as a rail service in a rural area, may nevertheless benefit from the existence of the service. The benefit they derive stems from the potential availability of an alternative form of transport as a form of insurance in situations where their own customary mode of transport is not available. In this case the surplus derived by examination of actual demand functions is an underestimate of the potential loss through withdrawal. Once again, one's judgement must be

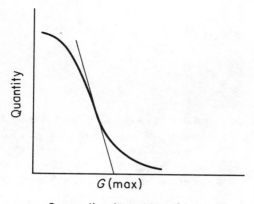

Generalised cost per journey

Figure 11.5

that whilst this is an interesting concept it probably has little relevance in the urban context, although it may be more important in rural conditions. Moreover, estimating the additional benefits from this source would present major practical difficulties.

CHAPTER TWELVE

Conclusion

The validity or efficiency of an appraisal process may be defined as the extent to which it provides good estimates of the gain to society from alternative courses of action. We consider the validity of the urban transport appraisal process described in earlier chapters in terms of the validity of the constituent elements as they have been described.

Forecasting

The efficiency of the forecasting process may be defined as the extent to which the modelling methods are able to predict the changes in travel costs and behaviour which result from policy changes and the operation of exogenous factors such as changes in people's incomes. A test of the efficiency of forecasts ultimately involves a comparison between 'forecast' and 'actual' behaviour in response to change. But, as has been emphasised at many points in the preceding discussion, the forecasting models used in urban transport appraisal have rarely been subjected to a validation process of this kind. Instead, validation has been based on the extent to which the model is able to reproduce an observed pattern of behaviour at a point in time.

To the extent that validation of the forecasting models is of this limited character, then we can be no more than agnostic about its efficiency in a forecasting context. It must, of course, be admitted that a thoroughgoing validation of the entire process would not be an easy matter. However, the efficiency of individual aspects of the process such as the stability of household trip-generation rates may be susceptible to relatively straightforward tests and this should be a research priority.

There are three other points we have noted about the potential validity of demand forecasting methods. First, it is commonly recognised that the outputs of forecasting exercises become more sensitive if they are predicting behaviour outside the observed range of values of the explanatory variables with which the model is estimated. Yet forecasting procedures are increasingly being confronted with this problem in the context of examining measures intended to increase the efficiency with which transport-network capacity is used. We might predict *a priori*, that transport users will respond to measures of this kind not only by switching their mode of travel, but perhaps by increasing car occupancies or by altering the time at which journeys are made. Current models offer very little direct scope for reactions of this kind because opportunities have not existed to observe the effects of relatively high levels of restraint on travel behaviour.

Second, it was noted at an early stage that forecasts of travel demand have usually assumed a given pattern of land uses. In the context of transportation studies, it has been further assumed that the land-use pattern is constant between the alternative options examined by the studies. It is obvious in a general way that because land-use forecasts are inputs to the forecasting process, the efficiency of the latter is related to the accuracy with which the land-use pattern is predicted. However, relatively little is known about the sensitivity of travel demand forecasts to variations in land-use patterns. For forecasts with a relatively short-term focus, the potential margin of error is small. But in the transportation study context, in which broad strategies are being examined in the context of a design year ten to fifteen years forward, it is important to know something of the degree of uncertainty attaching to land-use forecasts. The most important elements here are the forecasts of the volume and location of employment.

Finally, it should be noted that the procedures discussed earlier have been concerned with the production of forecasts of person journeys. Nothing has been said about any equivalent procedures for analysing and forecasting commercial vehicle journeys. In fact this topic has been very little explored. There has been some work on the analysis of commercial vehicle trip generation in terms of land uses but very little on the distribution of commercial vehicle journeys or the effects of changes in the average size of commercial vehicles and their carrying capacity on the volume of journeys made. Current practice in forecasting commercial vehicle movements often involves no more than the grossing up of an observed matrix of inter-zonal commercial vehicle journeys by a factor which might be based on forecast growth of G.N.P.

It seems unlikely that this limited treatment of a major class of vehicle movements will continue to be regarded as a satisfactory basis for forecasting. Factors such as the increasing public concern about the externalities imposed by heavy commercial vehicle movements in particular are likely to result in demands for more soundly based forecasts of commercial vehicle movements.

The problems associated with the specification of supply-side relationships to some extent parallel those on the demand side. For example, there is a relatively minor problem of the stability of speed–flow relationships, which is similar in nature to the major unresolved difficulty in demand forecasting. Otherwise, the main problems stem from the wider range of policies being examined by urban transport appraisal procedures. Because of prospective reductions in resource availability, increasing emphasis in the United Kingdom is being placed on the need to examine options involving relatively modest levels of expenditure, such as junction-improvement schemes or more extensive traffic-management measures. The extent to which policies of this kind can be represented in terms of the network description procedures used in transport planning is somewhat problematical.

Evaluation

The benefit assessment process described in Chapter 9 estimates benefits in terms of the costs to travellers of making trips in a 'do-nothing' (or before situation) and a 'do-something' (or after situation). Given the general form of the benefit expression, the benefits attributed to whatever policy or project is being evaluated are a function of travel behaviour and of the estimated costs of travel under the alternative conditions. A critical element in the latter is the value attached to the non-monetary costs of travel. A number of references were given in Chapter 5 to work which has been used to justify current U.K. practice in this field. However, there still remain a number of problems, in particular those relating to changes in time values as personal incomes increase.

The discussion on assessment criteria in Chapter 10 indicated that the design-year rate of return criterion which has often been used in transportation studies is inadequate as a guide both to the ranking of alternatives and their admissability (in the sense of their having a positive N.P.V.). The main difficulty with this criterion is that it relies on an estimate of the benefits made in respect of a single year as an indicator of benefits over the whole life of a set of capital projects. Shorter-term policy aimed at improving the use of transport systems may involve little or no capital expenditures. In this case, assessment of their worth may be validly based on a comparison of estimated annual benefits and operating cost changes, and the objections raised to the single-year criterion no longer apply.

Conclusion

The main conclusion to be drawn from this discussion is that the efficiency of the procedures by which urban transport projects and policies are appraised is not yet firmly established. The forecasting procedures, in particular, rest upon a number of hypotheses which have been tested only in respect of their ability to reproduce an observed situation. More research effort is therefore required to validate hypotheses about travel behaviour and also about the value people place on certain kinds of service-level improvement.

Finally, we should emphasise that appraisal procedures of the kind described in this book must be viewed as an element of a wider planning process. This covers the identification of problems, the generation of alternative policy and projects to meet them, the implementation of preferred options, and the monitoring of progress towards objectives. Clearly, the validity of appraisal procedures is, of itself, not sufficient to guarantee the validity of the over-all process. But the efficiency of the planning process does depend critically on the efficiency of the appraisal procedures embodied in it.

Notes and References

Chapter 1

1. See, for example, H. A. J. Green, *Consumer Theory* (London: Macmillan, 1976) ch. 12 for a discussion of the basic ideas behind the concept of time preference.
2. We have dealt here only with quantifiable benefits. Even if the present value of these does not exceed the capital cost, it may be judged that the unquantifiable benefits of a project (discussed at greater length in Chapter 11) may be sufficiently large to justify the project.

Chapter 2

1. Using the notation in R. G. D. Allen, *Mathematical Analysis for Economists* (London: Macmillan, 1960) p. 251.
2. H. L. I. Neuburger 'User Benefit in the Evaluation of Transport and Land-Use Plans', *Journal of Transport Economics and Policy*, Vol. 5, no. 1 (1971).
3. G. Kraft and M. Wohl, 'New Directions for Passenger Demand Analysis and Forecasting', *Transportation Research*, vol. 1, no. 3 (1967).
4. B. V. Martin, F. W. Memmott, and A. J. Bone, *Principles and Techniques of Predicting Future Urban Area Transportation* (Cambridge, Mass.: M. I. T. Press, 1965).
5. A simple numerical example may clarify this point. In order to analyse the demand for transport in a large urban area, the area might be divided up into a set of zones, so that the volume of zone-to-zone movements was the basic unit of analysis. Assume that the area was divided up into 100 zones; there would then be 4950 possible zone pairs. If there were two alternative modes of transport available between each pair of zones, then there would be 9900 potential mode-specific demand relationships. If, in addition, it was decided to analyse peak and off-peak movements separately, then the number of potential relationships would double again.

Chapter 3

1. An exception to this is Charles Rivers Associates, *A Disaggregated Behavioural Model of Urban Travel Demand*) Washington, D. C.: U. S. Department of Transportation, 1972).
2. M. L. Manheim, 'Practical Implications of Some Fundamental Properties of Travel Demand Models', *Highway Research Record 422*, (Washington D.C.:, H.R.B., 1973).

3. N. W. Mansfield, 'Recreational Trip Generation', *Journal of Transport Economics and Policy*, vol. 3, no. 2 (1969).

4. R. E. Quandt and W. J. Baumol, 'The Demand for Abstract Transport Models: Theory and Measurement', *Journal of Regional Science,* vol. 6, no. 2 (1966); see also R. E. Quandt and W. J. Baumol, 'The Demand for Abstract Transport Modes: Some Hopes', *Journal of Regional Science,* vol. 9, no. 1 (1969).

5. T. A. Domencich, G. Kraft and J. P. Valette, 'Estimation of Urban Passenger Travel Behaviour: An Economic Model', *Highway Research Record 238* (Washington D.C.: H.R.B., 1968).

Chapter 4

1. R. M. Mitchell and C. Rapkin, *Urban Traffic – A function of Land Use* (New York: Columbia University Press, 1964).

2. W. Y. Oi and P. W Shuldiner *'An Analysis of Urban Travel Demands',* Transportation Centre, Northwestern University (Evanston, Illinois: Northwestern University Press, 1962).

3. C. R. Fleet and S. R. Robertson, 'Trip Generation In the Transportation Planning Process', *Highway Research Record 240* (Washington D.C.: H.R.B., 1968).

4. Oi and Shuldiner, *Analysis of Urban Travel Demands*, table 65.

5. Ibid.

6. Ibid. table 52.

7. Ibid. table 5.

8. H. J. Wootton and G. W. Pick, 'A Model for Trips Generated by Households', *Journal of Transport Economics and Policy*, vol. 1, no. 2 (1967).

9. Extracted from Oi and Shuldiner, *Analysis of Urban Travel Demands*, table 11.

10. J. J. Bates and D. A. Quarmby, 'An Economic Method for Car Ownership Forecasting in Discrete Areas', *MAU Note 219* (London: Mathematical Advisory Unit, Department of the Environment, 1971).

11. J. C. Tanner, 'Forecasts of Vehicles and Traffic in Great Britain: 1974 Revision', *TRRL Laboratory Report 650* (London Transport and Road Research Laboratory, Department of the Environment, 1974).

12. J. F. Kain, 'A Contribution to the Urban Transportation Debate: an Econometric Model of Urban Residential and Travel Behaviour', *Review of Economics and Statistics*, vol. 66, no.1 (1964).

13. See, for example, 'Lincoln Land Use Transportation Study: Description of the Traffic Model and Computing Procedures', unpublished note (London: Department of the Environment, 1973).

Chapter 5

1. A. J. Harrison and D. A Quarmby, 'The Value of Time In Transport Planning: A Review', in *Theoretical and Practical Research on an Estimation of Time Saving* (Paris: E.C.M.T., 1969).

2. Ibid.

3. L. Goldberg, 'A Comparison of Transportation Plans for a Linear City', Paper presented to the International Conference on Operations Research and the Social Sciences, organised by the Operational Research Society, Cambridge, 1964.

4. See, for example, P. T. McIntosh and D. A. Quarmby, 'Generalised Costs, and the Estimation of Movement Costs and Benefits in Transport Planning', *MAU Note 179* (London: Mathematical Advisory Unit, Department of Environment, 1970).

5. See, for example, LGORU, 'Planning for the Work Journey', *Report NC. 67* (Reading: LGORU, 1973).

6. D. A. Quarmby 'Choice of Travel Mode for the Journey to Work', *Journal of Transport Economics and Policy,* vol. 1, no. 3 (1967).

7. See, for example, LGORU, 'Planning for the Work Journey'.

8. P. B. Goodwin, 'Generalised Time and the Problem of Equity in Transport Studies', *Transportation*, vol. 3, no. 1 (1974).

9. McIntosh and Quarmby, 'Generalised Costs, and The Estimation of Movement Costs and Benefits'.

10. D. J. Wagon and A. G Wilson, 'The Mathematical Model', *Technical Working Paper No. 5* (Manchester: SELNEC Transport Study, 1971).

11. T. A. Domencich, G. Kraft and J. P Valette 'Estimation of Passenger Travel Behaviour: An Economic Demand Model', *Highway Research Record 238* (Washington, D.C.: H.R.B., 1968).

Chapter 6

1. A number of such methods are described in W. Y. Oi and P. W. Schuldiner, *An Analysis of Urban Travel Demands,* Transportation Centre, Northwestern University (Evanston, Illinois: Northwestern University Press, 1962).

2. The single-stage model 'explains' both trip generation and model split as well as trip distribution.

3. A. G. Wilson, 'Advances and Problems in Distribution Modelling', *Transportation Research*, vol. 4, no. 1 (1970).

4. A. G. Wilson, 'A Statistical Theory of Spatial Distribution Models', *Transportation Research,* vol. 1 (1967) pp. 253 – 70; or A. G. Wilson, 'The Use of Entropy Maximising Methods in the Theory of Trip Distribution, Mode Split and Route Split', *Journal of Transport Economics and Policy,* vol. 3, no. 1 (1969).

5. Ibid.

6. A. G. Wilson, A. F. Hawkins, G. J. Hill and D. J. Wagon, 'Calibration and Testing of the SELNEC Transport Model', *Regional Studies*, vol. 3, no. 4 (1969).

7. See, for example, A. W. Evans, 'A General Theory of the Allocation of Time', unpublished paper, University of Glasgow (1969); or G. S. Becker, 'A Theory of the Allocation of Time', *Economic Journal*, vol. 75, no. 3 (1965).

8. M. E. Beesley, 'Motorways in London and Transport Planning', *Environment and Planning*, vol. 2, no. 1 (1970).

Chapter 7

1. A. G. Wilson, A. F. Hawkins, G. J. Hill and D. J. Wagon, 'Calibration and Testing of the SELNEC Transport Model', *Regional Studies*, vol. 2, no. 4 (1969).
2. This procedure in principle allows for the incorporation of a new mode on a subset of $i-j$ pairs.
3. A. G. Wilson, 'The Use of Entropy Maximising Methods in the Theory of Trip Distribution, Mode Split, and Route Split', *Journal of Transport Economics and Policy*, vol. 3, no. 1 (1969).
4. D. Brand, 'Travel Demand Forecasting: Some Foundations and a Review', in 'Urban Travel Demand Forecasting', *Special Report 143* (Washington, D.C.: H.R.B., 1972).
5. R. D. Luce, *Individual Choice Behaviour* (New York: Wiley, 1959).
6. See, for example, P. L. Watson, *The Value of Time: Behavioural Modal Choice* (Lexington, Mass: D. C. Heath, 1974).
7. See, for example, Local Government Operational Research Unit, 'Predicting Multi-Mode Choice', *Report C139* (Reading: LGORU, 1973).
8. F. X. De Donnea, 'Consumer Behaviour, Transport Mode Choice and Value of Time, Some Micro-Economic Models', *Regional and Urban Economics, Operation Methods*, vol. 1, no. 4 (1972).
9. D. McFadden, 'The Measurement of Urban Travel Demand', *Journal of Public Economics*, vol. 3, no. 3 (1974).

Chapter 8

1. Freeman, Fox, Wilbur Smith and Associates, *London Transportation Study Phase 3* (Greater London Council, 1968).
2. See, for example, A. A. Walters, 'The Theory and Measurement of Private and Social Costs of Highway Congestion', *Econometrica*, vol. 29 (1961) pp. 676–99.
3. H. L. I. Neuburger, 'The Economics of Heavily Congested Roads', *Transportation Research*, vol. 5 (1971) pp. 283–92.
4. 'Speed–Flow Relationships for Use in Transportation Studies', *Transportation Studies Advice Note 1A*, Urban Project Appraisal Directorate (London:Department of the Environment, undated).
5. G. L. Stephens and R. N. Cox, 'The Hammersmith Assignment Model', *Proceedings of a Seminar on Urban Traffic Models* (London: P.T.R.C., 1972).
6. R. F. F. Dawson, 'Vehicle Operating Costs and Costs of Road Accidents in 1967', *Road Research Technical Note 360* (London: Ministry of Transport, 1968).
7. J. R. Burrell, 'Multiple Route Assignment and its Application to Capacity Restraint', *Proceedings of the Fourth International Symposium on the Theory of Traffic Flow* (Karlsruhe, 1968); and V. Outram, 'Assignment Techniques', *MAU Note 237*, Mathematical Advisory Unit (London:Department of the Environment, 1972).

8. See, for example, Freeman, Fox, Wilbur Smith and Associates, *Transportation Analysis Programs* (London, 1967).

9. Much of the material here is derived from Neuburger, 'The Economics of Heavily Congested Roads'.

Chapter 9

1. A. Marshall, *Principles of Economics*, 8th edn (London: Macmillan, 1920).

2. J. R. Hicks, *A Revision of Demand Theory* (Oxford University Press, 1956); see also E. J. Mishan, *Cost-Benefit Analysis* (London: Unwin, 1971); or S. Glaister, 'Generalised Consumer Surplus and Public Transport Pricing', *Economic Journal*, vol. 84 (1974) pp. 849–67.

3. See, for example, M. E. Burns, 'A Note on the Concept and Measure of Consumer's Surplus', *American Economic Review*, vol. 63 (1973) pp. 335–44.

4. H. Hotelling, 'The General Welfare in Relation to Problems of Taxation and of Railway and Utility Rates', *Econometrica*, vol. 6 (1938) pp. 242–69.

5. C. D. Foster and H. L. I. Neuburger, 'The Ambiguity of the Consumer's Surplus Measure of Welfare Change', *Oxford Economic Papers*, vol. 26 (1974) pp. 66–77.

6. D. Reaume, 'Cost–Benefit Techniques and Consumer Surplus: A Clarificatory Analysis', *Public Finance*, vol. 29, no. 2 (1974).

7. H. L. I. Neuburger, 'Perceived Cost', *Environment and Planning*, vol. 3, no. 1 (1971).

8. This is a slight oversimplification. We are really assuming that measured transport-sector benefits are a full estimate of the benefits of transport-sector price changes to the economy.

9. See, for example, P. T. McIntosh and D. A. Quarmby, 'Generalised Costs and the Estimation of Movement Costs and Benefits in Transport Planning', *MAU Note 179*, Mathematical Advisory Unit (London: Department of the Environment, 1970).

10. W. J. Baumol and D. F. Bradford, 'Optimal Departures from Marginal Cost Pricing', *American Economic Review*, vol. 60 (1970) pp. 265–83.

11. N. Lichfield, 'Economics in Town Planning', *Town Planning Review*, vol. 38 (1968) pp. 5–20.

Chapter 10

1. S. A. Marglin, *Approaches to Dynamic Investment Planning* (Amsterdam: North–Holland, 1963).

2. A major exception was the London Transportation Study which examined highway strategies embodying widely different levels of expenditure.

3. I. S. Jones, 'Option Design and Economic Evaluation in Transportation Studies', paper presented to the P.T.R.C. Conference, University of Warwick (1974).

Chapter 11

1. See, for example, E. J. Mishan, *Cost – Benefit Analysis* (London: Unwin, 1971).

2. See, for example, A. Lassiere, 'The Environmental Evaluation of Transport Plans' (London: H.M.S.O., 1976).

3. M. Hill, 'A Goals Achievement Matrix for Evaluating Alternative Plans', *Journal of the American Institute of Planners*, vol. 34, no. 1 (1968).

4. See I. M. D. Little, *A Critique of Welfare Economics* (Oxford University Press, 1957); or T. Scitovsky, 'A Note on Welfare Propositions in Economics', *Review of Economic Studies*, vol. 9 (1941) pp. 77 – 88.

5. I. S. Jones, 'Option Design and Economic Evaluation in Transportation Studies', paper presented to the P.T.R.C. Conference, University of Warwick (1974).

6. See, for example, Greater London Council, *A Study of Supplementary Licensing* (London: County Hall, 1976).

7. R. Schmalensee, 'Option Demand and Consumer's Surplus: Valuing Price Changes under Uncertainty', *American Economic Review*, vol. 62, no. 4 (1972).

Index